OUR FRIEND JOE

D0759971

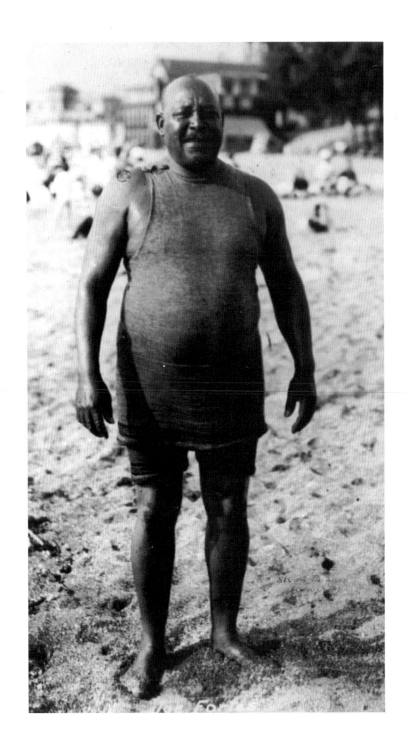

Our Friend Joe

THE JOE FORTES STORY

Lisa Anne Smith &
Barbara Rogers

Enjoy meeting Joe!
Lisa Smith

RONSDALE PRESS

OUR FRIEND JOE
Copyright © 2012 Lisa Anne Smith & Barbara Rogers

All rights reserved. No part of this publication may be reproduced, stored in a retrieval system, or transmitted, in any form or by any means, without prior written permission of the publisher, or, in Canada, in the case of photocopying or other reprographic copying, a licence from Access Copyright (the Canadian Copyright Licensing Agency).

RONSDALE PRESS
3350 West 21st Avenue
Vancouver, B.C. Canada V6S 1G7
www.ronsdalepress.com

Typesetting: Julie Cochrane, in Granjon 11.5 pt on 16
Cover Design: Julie Cochrane
Front Cover Photo: Portrait of Joe Fortes, c. 1910
    (Vancouver Public Library Accession #39420A)
Frontispiece: Joe on duty at English Bay beach, c. 1915. (CVA, Port P114.1)
Paper: Ancient Forest Friendly Rolland Enviro Satin FSC Recycled—
    100% post-consumer waste, totally chlorine-free and acid-free.

Ronsdale Press wishes to thank the following for their support of its publishing program: the Canada Council for the Arts, the Government of Canada through the Canada Book Fund, the British Columbia Arts Council, and the Province of British Columbia through the British Columbia Book Publishing Tax Credit program.

Library and Archives Canada Cataloguing in Publication

Smith, Lisa, 1959–
    Our friend Joe: the Joe Fortes story / Lisa Anne Smith & Barbara Rogers.

Includes bibliographical references and index.
Issued also in electronic format.
ISBN 978-1-55380-146-7

    1. Fortes, Joe. 2. Lifeguards—British Columbia—Vancouver—Biography.
I. Rogers, Barbara, 1936– II. Title.

GV838.F67S65 2012   797.20092   C2011-906960-1

At Ronsdale Press we are committed to protecting the environment. To this end we are working with Canopy (formerly Markets Initiative) and printers to phase out our use of paper produced from ancient forests. This book is one step towards that goal.

Printed in Canada by Marquis Book Printing, Montreal, Quebec

for Joe
and others who have
loved the water

CONTENTS

ACKNOWLEDGEMENTS

There are many individuals that we would like to thank for helping us to tell Joe's story. First and foremost, many thanks to Ronald Hatch and the staff of Ronsdale Press for their support, professionalism and most welcome guidance during this project. The creative suggestions and eagle-eyed editing skills of Noah Moscovitch, Erinna Gilkison and Deirdre Salisbury brought life to the text and accuracy to the content in ways unforeseen. Julie Cochrane developed the lovely cover concept, giving Joe a distinctive swagger in his studio photo.

Staff of Vancouver City Archives, notably archivist Megan Schlase, helped us to navigate untold kilometres of microfilm and trundled out the weighty (pre-online) Major Matthews volumes on many an occasion. Vancouver Public Library Special Collections was a treasure trove of information. Librarian Andrew Martin and library technician Kim McCarthy were of particular help in finding elusive Joe articles and photos from days gone by. The staff of the Joe Fortes Branch Library, notably Michelle Cobban and former staff member Mary Jane Culbert, were also of invaluable assistance.

When microfilmed copies became too illegible to decipher, the staff of the Provincial Legislative Library in Victoria was most helpful in providing access to original issues of early Vancouver newspapers. Carrie Schmidt, librarian archivist with the Vancouver Maritime Museum, is to be commended for her assistance in tracking down photographs of the *Robert Kerr*. Angela Burghard was of help in obtaining historical data relating to Holy Rosary Cathedral. Staff of the Vancouver Police Museum provided us with informative documentation relating to Joe's special constable duties. Iline Gronland and Peter Claydon of the B.C. Genealogical Society contributed their valuable expertise during the census research.

A big overseas thank-you goes to "the Liverpool crew"—researcher Roger Hull of the Liverpool Record Office, historian Tom Slemen, and Liverpool History Society members Ernest Nugent and Kathy Proctor—for their assistance in helping us to track Joe's Liverpool years. Special thanks to Carl Berkley, as well, for his fascinating and vivid description of swimming across the River Mersey.

Conservation and curatorial staff at the Museum of Vancouver and Native Daughters of B.C. Post #1 have taken good care over the years to ensure that a small collection of "Joe artifacts" remains in pristine condition. We are fortunate that through their efforts we can continue to enjoy these treasures. In a 1985 dedication ceremony for the Joe Fortes Seafood and Chop House restaurant, guests who had known Joe were invited to share their personal recollections—many of which can be found in this book. A big thank-you goes to restaurateur Bud Kanke, for his vision to perpetuate Joe's story.

The bi-weekly Wednesday night Writer's club meetings with Norma Dixon, Nora Schubert, Dorothy Macey and Nixie the cat were much looked forward to, as we put *Our Friend Joe* under the microscope, page by page. Special thanks go to Eileen Boberg, Doug, Hillary and Bobby Smith for awesome moral and technical support! Lastly, a warm hug of thanks goes to Barbara Howard of Joe's Vancouver "family," for sharing her memorabilia and recollections with us.

We trust that you will enjoy getting to know Joe Fortes through these pages. We acknowledge that there are still many questions unanswered, many stories untold. Much work remains to decode satisfactorily the mystery that is Joe. *Our Friend Joe* is a work in progress that perhaps may awaken some long buried memories—or open some long closed steamer trunks. If you have a "Joe story" that you wouldn't mind sharing, we would greatly appreciate hearing from you.

February 7, 1922

The rowboat edged its way up rain-soaked Dunsmuir Street. Securely tied upon the bed of a Ford Model T pickup, the boat was heaped with brilliant arrangements of flowers and evergreen boughs freshly cut from Stanley Park. Ahead of the truck, a hearse was conveying the body of Seraphim Joseph Fortes to the stone steps of Holy Rosary Cathedral. The coffin could barely be glimpsed between the rows of uniformed police guardsmen who strode alongside the vehicle. It was the rowboat that brought tears to the eyes of many in the crowd of thousands who had converged upon downtown Vancouver. Only months earlier, that very same boat had plied the waters off English Bay beach, Joe Fortes pulling hard at the oars, his muscular arms gleaming in the summer sun, his rich Trinidadian voice bellowing out orders: "Kick yo' feet chile! Don' you stop kickin' or you'll get nowhere fast!"

Joe Fortes was a Vancouver legend. Everyone, from the wealthiest businessman on Shaughnessy Heights to the back-alley hobo of the city's grittiest neighbourhoods, knew of Joe. There was always a story in the paper of another of Joe's rescues at English Bay. Officially, he was credited with saving twenty-six people from drowning—unofficially, many more.[1] Joe Fortes. Shipwrecked sailor. Little education. No formal training in lifesaving, child psychology or criminology. Yet Joe became Vancouver's first official swimming instructor, lifeguard and a special constable, hired by the City of Vancouver to maintain law and order at English Bay. He was a father figure to generations of Vancouver children, and a friend to many more. And now, on this cold, late-winter morning, people gathered along the funeral procession route to Holy Rosary Cathedral to say goodbye to Joe.

CHAPTER 1

Trinidadian Roots

For a man who was to have such a profound impact on the youth of Vancouver, Joe's own childhood is shrouded in mystery. Despite much research, no birth certificate or record has ever been found. In an 1891 Canada census, Joe gave his birthplace as Barbados.[1] A 1901 census listed Trinidad as his birthplace.[2] A 1911 census offered nothing more definitive than "West Indies."[3] There continues to be some debate over Joe's origin, but in all early interviews, he confirmed his birthplace and childhood home as Trinidad. An exact birthdate is also hard to establish—was it February 9, 1863? Or was it 1865? Again the dates in the censuses conflict. What we do know is that Joe's West Indian father was a sugar plantation worker, his mother a woman of Spanish ancestry. This mixed race parentage resulted in Joe's skin being a tone of chestnut brown, rather than the typically darker colouration of West Indians.

Further information about Joe's background may be gained through a short study of Trinidad's history. Discovered by Christopher Columbus in 1498, Trinidad lies thirteen miles north of the Venezuelan coast. For many years the island languished under Spanish governance. The land was covered with a nearly impenetrable forest of tropical vegetation. Trinidad's wet season extends from June through December, pummelling the island with heavy rains—Joe was obviously well-prepared for Vancouver's overcast skies. Any semblance of industry amounted to little more than a scattering of small farms. In 1783, observing a largely Amerindian population of less than three thousand, the Spanish crown offered thirty-two acres of free land to white colonists and half that amount to "free Negroes" and persons of colour. Conditionally, each new arrival had to be Roman Catholic and from a country friendly to Spain.[4] So began a slow but steady colonization of Trinidad. It is quite possible that some of Joe's maternal ancestors were among those who accepted the generous Spanish offer.

On February 18, 1797, Spanish rule abruptly ended when Governor José María Chacón surrendered to a British fleet of eighteen warships under the command of Sir Ralph Abercromby. By 1802, a widely diverse Trinidad populace was formally ceded to the United Kingdom. Like most Trinidadians in the nineteenth century, Joe proudly considered himself British to the core.

Trade vessels from Liverpool and Southampton, similar to the ones Joe would sail on in his teenage years, nosed up to the Port of Spain dockyards in ever-increasing numbers as demand for

Caribbean products grew. Sugar, the white gold that had fast become a staple on European dining tables, was particularly sought after. At the time of succession, about 150 sugar estates were established along the drier west coast of Trinidad. By mid-century, with generous British financing, sugar was at peak production, never falling below twenty thousand tons per year. In 1866, a record forty thousand tons of sugar was harvested, and plantation owners basked in the wealth.[5] Joe grew up in a world that revolved around the sugar industry.

Under the leadership of Lord Harris, governor of Trinidad from 1846 to 1854, the island had been divided into eight counties, each of which was subdivided into wards. Although little is known of Joe's educational background, he probably attended one of the "ward schools" that had been established for primary age students. Education in nineteenth-century Trinidad was a haphazard process, often dictated by work obligations in the cane fields or the ability to navigate mud-laden roads to the school-house during the wet season. It is said that a Trinidadian teacher spent more time luxuriating in a hammock than in front of a classroom while absent pupils helped with the harvest.[6] As a subject of the British crown, Joe would have been taught in English, recognized as the official language of Trinidad since the 1802 succession. Upon completion of his primary studies, Joe would have been faced with a simple decision—attend one of the two island colleges, or continue his secondary education abroad.

During his teenage years, Joe may have attended St Mary's College, the sole institution for young Catholics in 1870s Trinidad. The alternative, Protestant faith–based Queen's Collegiate School, had been angrily condemned by the Roman Catholic Archbishop Ferdinand English some years earlier. St. Mary's College, opened in 1863, offered boarders and day students courses in Latin, Greek, English, French, Spanish, history, ancient and modern geography, science, mathematics and music. The two official languages of the school were English and French. Boarders were required to pay 192 Trinidad and Tobago dollars per year and dayboys, students who returned home each evening, paid seventy-two Trinidad and Tobago dollars. The Sunday or dress uniform was black, while the weekday uniform included grey pants and a straw boater. Life at St Mary's was not easy. Discipline was severe, with floggings administered regularly for misbehaviour. The cause of some of the misbehaviour was the intense rivalry between the island-born students and those who had come across the water from Venezuela.[7]

By his own admission Joe was not a scholarly individual, in contrast to his younger brother who was being groomed to study medicine abroad. He had learned cursive handwriting but his letters were awkward and stilted. The two examples of Joe's penmanship that can be found today on Vancouver City Archives microfiche—an autographed note and a (presumed) reference to a photograph—are written in a crude form of Spanish, suggesting that he may have been educated partly at home by his mother or another individual of Hispanic origin. In 1943, City Archivist Major James Skitt Matthews attempted to decipher the carefully preserved originals. The well-meaning Major scrawled his own annotations and theories beneath Joe's handwriting:

> "An inquiry esta de Serafim Fortes"—What I think has happened is this. Some one of his friends has asked him for an autograph and to please them he has done his best. Not being a good scholar he did the best he could, and probably tried to say "This is a relic (or souvenir) of Seraphim Fortes," ie. Joe Fortes of English Bay.
>
> J.S. Matthews, 8 July 1943[8]

The second note was given similar treatment:

"esta vista Bo baca"—It may be that he is intending to say that the view of English Bay from his cottage on Beach Avenue, just west of his monument in Alexander Park. His cottage was between Beach Avenue and the sandy shore.

J.S. Matthews, 8 July 1943

Whatever he lacked in academic capabilities, it would soon become clear that Joe was an athlete at heart. Swimming, the sport for which Joe would one day become renowned, was a surprisingly obscure pastime in nineteenth-century Trinidad. Public swimming pools were non-existent, and the local beaches around Port of Spain were thick with mud and home to a thriving number of prickly sea urchins and stingrays. North shore surf was treacherous, with strong undertows that could render even the most capable swimmers helpless mere feet from shore.

Recreational opportunities on the whole were scarce for natural athletes like Joe. Queen's Park Savannah, originally a 260-acre plot of sugar land on the outskirts of Port of Spain, was purchased from the Peschier family in 1817 by the town council. By 1854, the park featured a horse-racing oval and grandstand, but pitches for football, rugby and cricket were yet to be realized. Did Joe develop his rowing prowess on the fringes of Caroni Swamp at sundown, enjoying the phenomenon of scarlet ibises flocking to roost atop the mangrove trees? One can only surmise. But by the age of seventeen, Joe was ready for life beyond the confines of Trinidad.

CHAPTER 2

Liverpool Years

Joe departed Trinidad with mixed emotions. It is suspected that there was a serious rift with his father,[1] perhaps fostered by Joe's lack of interest in pursuing further studies in England— a rite of passage for young Trinidadian men of some means. On the other hand, his mother gave Joe her blessing, and bestowed upon her son words of advice that he would recall throughout his life: "You live so that you look everyone in the face, and then you will be afraid of nothing and nobody."[2] Well aware that she might never see him again, she added, "Never forget to whom you belong, and always be straight and honest."[3]

Joe took employment as a deckhand aboard a brigantine loaded with sugar and headed to Swansea, Wales. From there it was on to Liverpool, then with general cargo back across the Atlantic to Rio de Janeiro and Buenos Aires. Joe's third crossing took him to Amsterdam and then once again to Liverpool. It was Liverpool that seemed to capture Joe's imagination most, and it was in Liverpool where he decided to settle in the early days of the 1880s.[4]

Liverpool, the legendary port city sprawled along the banks of the River Mersey in the heart of England's industrialized Midlands, was a dramatic sight for any new arrival. The harbour was a forest of masts, testimony to the thriving shipping industry of the day. Pedestrians jockeyed for position amidst streets jammed with carriages, omnibuses, lorries, carts and drays. Albert Dock, a collection of buildings and warehouses opened in 1846 by Prince Albert, dominated the skyline. The structure, built from cast iron, brick and stone, was the world's first fire-proof dock complex and a marvel of engineering. Despite these wonders, it was another riverfront structure that transfixed Joe, and inspired his decision to stay in Liverpool: St. George's Pier Head Public Baths.

For all its grandeur, Liverpool had long been a city of slums and deprivation. Cholera outbreaks were common as a result of poor sanitation. In an effort to combat the disease and improve sanitation, a public bath complex, including a swimming pool, was opened on June 8, 1829, in the very heart of Liverpool. The exterior of St. George's Pier Head Baths was constructed in the tradition of Victorian elegance, with columns and a central clock tower. At a cost in excess of thirty thousand pounds, the baths were an expensive undertaking, and not initially successful in the city's fight to control cholera. In the 1832 cholera pandemic over fifteen hundred lives were lost in Liverpool.

The potato famine of 1845 triggered a flood of Irish migration into Liverpool, further worsening the living conditions, and by the time of Joe's arrival some thirty-five years later, the city was still rife with poverty and overcrowding—but thanks to a string of public baths and wash houses, sanitation had vastly improved.

Joe's place of residence in Liverpool remains unknown; his name does not appear in any street directory or census of the early 1880s. A large black community had established itself around the south docklands area, and the Elder Dempster shipping line ran a hostel for black sailors. As sugar refineries were coming into their heyday, Joe may have boarded with a contact through his father's work. Perhaps he earned his accommodation through odd jobs at one of the city's elite hotels—or found rudimentary lodging in one of the myriad courtyard dwellings or cellars that served as shelter for the city's poorer inhabitants. Legislation had been passed to demolish Liverpool's notorious slum districts, but demand for new housing fast outpaced the supply.

Regardless of where he bedded down at the end of the day, Joe spent a great many of his waking hours at St. George's Pier Head Public Baths. He found employment as an attendant and, in his off-duty hours, rapidly honed his natural talent for swimming.[5] The baths, as described in Liverpool archival records, were "appropriated to gentlemen at the northern end and to ladies at the southern extremity of the building; and a cold plunge bath, with convenient dressing rooms, situated in each compartment. A spacious tank beneath the centre of the building, containing upwards of 800 tons, receives the water from the river at high tide; from this reservoir it is forced, by means of a steam engine, into a capacious filter, and thence conveyed, perfectly pure and clear as crystal, through pipes, into the respective baths through which it is constantly flowing in a fresh current."[6]

Swimming was enjoying a dramatic increase in popularity in

Joe discovers his passion for swimming at St. George's Pier Head Public Baths, c. 1907. (LIVERPOOL PUBLIC RECORDS OFFICE, NO. 250)

the United Kingdom. Historically, the sport had been widely frowned upon throughout Europe. People believed that water spread plague and other diseases. Those daring enough to defy this logic employed an ungainly form of side stroke or breast-stroke that kept the face well out of the water. Widely organized swimming championships began in the 1870s. At the time there were no separate events for different strokes, and swimmers competed in wild free-for-alls, incorporating any style that suited their preference. It wasn't until Londoner John Trudgen as-tounded his competitors with a distinctive double overarm stroke at a race on August 11, 1873, that swimming truly began to evolve. The powerful "trudgen," a precursor to the modern-day crawl, was the preferred stroke of Joe's day. Experimentation was also well underway with side-to-side rolls, submerging one's chest and face in the water to minimize frontal resistance, and more efficient timing of kicks. Joe took lessons from one of the more notable instructors and quickly became a skilful swimmer and diver. His swimming prowess soon caught the eye of other pool regulars, and a tall Church of England minister came up to Joe one day with an interesting challenge.

"My boy," he said, "you are only a lad, but I believe that you will be a great swimmer. We will pay ten shillings to the boy who can get the bunghole out of the big tank. You must try."

The "bunghole" to which the minister referred was a plug at the bottom of the men's forty-five by twenty-seven foot tank. Both the men's and women's tanks were routinely emptied for cleaning, requiring an individual to inhale a great gulp of air, dive to the bottom and draw upon every ounce of muscle power to haul out the heavy plug. No easy task even for the most seasoned of swimmers.

"There's an Austrian in for it, thinks he's everything, and you must show him he's not!" the minister told Joe.

Feeling the stirring of his British pride, Joe nodded that he would try, and in seemingly no time at all, emerged from the water with the plug.

"I'll give you a pound, because you took something off that Austrian's head!" the minister said, laughing heartily.[7]

One summer night in 1881, Joe swam 1,312 yards across the River Mersey, allegedly to visit a young Irish girl. Whether he sought to impress his lady friend or test his endurance is open to conjecture. The remarkable feat was witnessed by Captain Wagstaff, an elderly member of Liverpool's high society and once an athlete in his own right. Captain Wagstaff was an honorary member of Liverpool's secret "Daredevil Club," which met the first Thursday evening of every month at luxurious premises on the fashionable Duke Street. The sole aim of the Daredevil Club, composed of approximately sixty individuals from all walks of life, was to engage in a wide variety of devil-may-care stunts and madcap schemes—always challenging, occasionally unlawful, and frequently for cash rewards. At the August 1881 meeting, one member of the club challenged any other member "to swim across the River Mersey in the dead of night, the fastest swimmer to be awarded a sum of no less than a thousand guineas."[8] Gasps of astonishment reverberated through the room. Two swimmers signed up almost immediately—John McNaughten and Zalech Goldstein, the bravado-filled Austrian. Captain Wagstaff carefully maintained a deadpan expression, while his mind churned with recollections of the young Trinidadian sailor he had so recently witnessed accomplishing the very feat now being wagered upon. A few days later, the captain tracked down Joe, paid his club membership fee and entered him in the cross-Mersey race.

Joe's admittance to the Daredevil Club caused a certain degree of consternation. Joe was *black*. Black people were not readily welcome amidst Liverpool elite. Nevertheless, Joe took his place alongside McNaughten and Goldstein at the stroke of midnight on August 31, 1881, at the landing stage of Queen's Dock. Minutes after the three men dove into the freezing waters, John McNaughten lost his nerve and began swimming back. Joe and Zalech continued, oblivious to the angry-looking policeman who was hauling John into a rowboat. Joe struck out hard and quickly gained the lead. Swimming the Mersey was not for the faint of heart at any time of day: the waters were thick with the taste and stench of industrial effluent, and a fierce current was only moderately slackened by the full tide. Within twenty-five minutes, Joe clambered up on the Birkenhead shore. Zalech was calling out of the darkness some distance behind that he was cramping up. Without hesitation Joe dived back into the water and rescued his adversary. The feat accomplished, Joe was the toast of the hour in the plush surroundings of the Daredevil Club. By virtue of financing Joe's membership fee, Captain Wagstaff successfully negotiated his claim on half of Joe's thousand-guinea prize. He would soon lose a portion in hush money, paid to silence the police officer who was planning to charge the three swimmers with trespass after rescuing John McNaughten.

In later years, Joe acknowledged that his River Mersey swims were foolhardy, but "being in full blood" his teenage mind knew no fear.[9] The midnight race solidified his reputation as a swimming sensation, and he went on to dazzle audiences with his talent at exhibition performances in Blackpool. He was presented with a medal and floral bouquet from the pretty blond daughter of the Lord Mayor of Liverpool—"she sure was a little peach," he would often fondly recall.[10]

A tour through southern France soon followed, in the company of friends from an international organization known as the Order of Good Templars. Good Templar Lodges were a form of Freemasonry, open to any and all individuals regardless of race or gender. Templar Brothers and Sisters were dedicated to the plight of those who had fallen victim to the temptations of alcohol. Joe, having been raised in the Catholic faith, was inspired by the founding principles of Good Templary: "Total Abstinence for the Individual and Total Prohibition for the State."[11] By the late nineteenth century over 1,450,000 individuals throughout the United Kingdom had taken the Good Templary "Total

Abstinence Pledge." Hospitals, orphanages and the Royal National Lifeboat Institution were all beneficiaries of the Templars' work.

While in Liverpool, Joe would likely have attended worship services at St. Mary's Edmund Street Roman Catholic Church, located mere blocks from the Pier Head. Built in 1845 to hold three thousand parishioners, St. Mary's was the bastion for Catholic faith in nineteenth-century Liverpool. During the height of the potato famine, attendance doubled and worshippers jammed the aisles and vestibules as Irish Catholics flooded into the otherwise predominantly Church of England city. In 1883, the church lay directly in the path of a planned Liverpool Exchange railway station expansion. Parishioners took it upon themselves to relocate St. Mary's piece by piece to nearby Highfield Street.[12] One can well imagine the strong and youthful Joe taking great delight in helping to move the heaviest slabs of masonry.

In his own words, Joe came to know Liverpool "like a book" during his time there. He would have strolled through the stone-vaulted pavement arcades of the Goree Piazza, perhaps watched a cricket match or rented a rowboat in Sefton Park. He may have paused for contemplation in the shadows of the seventeenth-century town hall, constructed with financial proceeds from Liverpool's involvement in the slave trade. He would have joined the crowds watching in awe at dockside as the Cunard Line's S.S. *Servia*, the second largest ship in the world and the first to feature electric lighting, set out on its maiden voyage to New York. By all appearances, Joe greatly enjoyed his Liverpool days, but by the fall of 1884 it seems that his wanderlust was beckoning once again.

CHAPTER 3

Aboard the *Robert Kerr*

On the morning of October 2, 1884, the steam tug *Knight of St. John* towed the *Robert Kerr* through a steady drizzle westward down the River Mersey. Among a crew of eleven, Able-Bodied Seaman Seraphim Fortes attended to his assigned tasks. A Hudson's Bay Company merchant vessel, the *Robert Kerr* had been plying the trade-run between Britain and the Americas since its construction in Quebec in 1866.[1] On this voyage, a cargo load of coal was destined for Panama City. At 190 feet in length, the *Kerr* was easily dwarfed by the modern steam-driven giants of the Cunard and White Star lines. The glorious era of the tall sailing ships was drawing to a close, but a gradually decreasing number of weathered old beauties, such as the *Robert Kerr*, stubbornly maintained a dying tradition.

By eleven thirty in the evening, the notorious gales of the Irish Sea had whipped up, and the *Robert Kerr* was subjected to the first of what would be an ongoing barrage of North Atlantic storms. Captain Edward Edwards, a well-seasoned veteran of such conditions, issued orders for a steady southwesterly course. In the wildly rocking forward cabin, First Mate John Richardson somehow maintained a steady hand as he recorded, in perfectly legible script, the day-to-day particulars of the voyage: "November 19th, 1884—Gale increasing, mountainous seas, ship labouring heavily, mid to whole gale force squalls with very heavy thunder and lightning."[2] The journal continues: "December 7th, 1884—Gale continuing, very high sea having broken up a lot of things about the decks such as ladders, light screen, doors, etc."[3]

Apparently the storms were taken in stride as most log entries describe, in a nonchalant, almost disinterested tone, the ongoing, routine shipboard chores. Joe and his crewmates busied themselves with mundane tasks such as repairing sails, attending to pumps, scrubbing the deck and taking their shift at two-hour watches.

As there were no scheduled ports of call between Liverpool and Panama City, food stores were carefully monitored for quantity and spoilage. Joe's typical meal aboard the *Robert Kerr* consisted of salt beef or pork, a soup or stew made from dried beans, a sea biscuit and limes to ward off scurvy.

During the week before Christmas, the *Robert Kerr* rounded Cape Horn:

December 18th, 1884—4 p.m. Hermit Island bore N.N.W. about 30 miles. 8 p.m. Diego Ramirez bore W. by N. 30 miles distant. Moderate gale with barometer falling rapidly. Took in and furled all topsail except lower. . . . Heavy sea, ship hove to on starboard tack, labouring heavily, shipping large quantities of water. . . . Seraphim on watch 6–8 p.m.[4]

December 19th, 1884—Latitude 57.32 degrees South. Hove to on starboard tack, heavy seas. Crew standing by. Pumps, lights and lookouts attended to. William Anderson threatened two times to hit me on the head with a Capstan bar. I reported it to the Captain.[5]

By December 22, the *Robert Kerr*'s journey around the Horn was complete, as first mention was made in the log of a shift to a northwest course.[6] December 25 was made "a general holiday, it being Christmas Day."[7] No doubt for Joe and his crewmates, the best Christmas present was the realization that warmer climes and calmer seas were short weeks ahead. A few of the men were becoming testy as the voyage wore on. William Anderson seemed to be particularly notorious for stirring up trouble: "January 2nd, 1885—Seraphim Fortes AB, came aft and reported that William Anderson AB had stuck a cotton hook into his cheek."[8]

There is no indication from the log entry as to whether or not Anderson was reported to the Captain for this misdemeanour. If the outbursts were triggered by sheer boredom, matters were about to get worse. By early February, the *Robert Kerr* had entered the becalmed region of the Pacific known as the doldrums. On February 2, recorded sailing distance was forty-four miles,[9] and February 3, twenty-two miles.[10] On February 6, at latitude 0.40 south, one could almost hear the onboard frustration as John Richardson scrawled "Calm, Calm, Calm"[11] in the logbook. The *Robert Kerr* had travelled only sixteen miles. Taking advantage of the near-motionless equatorial conditions, crewmen were sent over the ship's sides to scrub away barnacles and sea grass.

On February 28, the *Robert Kerr* "came to anchor in Panama Roads with 30 fathoms on port cable, furled all sail and cleared up decks."[12] It would be several more days before the ship would be towed further into Panama City harbour, which was jammed with vessels of every size and description. The Panama Canal Company, under the management of Frenchman Ferdinand Marie de Lesseps, was well into the preliminary stages of a phenomenal project—the digging of a navigable channel across the narrow isthmus between North and South America. Coal-powered steam dredges were already making steady progress in the eastern Culebra Cut. The *Robert Kerr*'s cargo load of coal would soon be put to good use. Joe and his crewmates worked hard for days on end, sending tons of coal down carpenter Thomas Jones' pre-assembled coal shoot and replacing the load with stone ballast. If Joe had any desire to view the workings of the Panama Canal Company, he may have well been advised to stay away as the interior jungles were rife with outbreaks of malaria and yellow fever.

May 5 saw the *Robert Kerr*'s departure "on a voyage from Panama to Victoria, Vancouver's Island."[13] For several uneventful weeks, the ship progressed steadily northward. On June 10, Joe was noted on the sick list—a first for him thus far in the voyage.[14] By June 15, he had recovered well enough to be on watch from four to six in the morning.[15] The first telltale entry in the first mate's log of a much worse affliction for another individual is dated July 15: "The Captain went on deck during the night and got wet. He is now complaining that his legs are swelling. He is rubbing them with turtle oil."[16]

A Welshman by birth, Captain Edwards had logged many years of experience in command at sea: the *Walton* from 1865 to 1872, the *Eurydice* from 1873 to 1881, and the *Robert Kerr* from

1882. At sixty-two years of age, he may have been looking forward to retirement, comfortable in the knowledge that he had run his ships at the highest standards of safety and efficiency. The logbook entries of John Richardson tell the rest of the story:

> July 16th—Captain is no better today but says his stomach is swelling. It has the appearance of dropsy.[17]

> July 17th—Captain is no better and says his complaint is inflammation of the kidneys. He is giving instructions to the steward for his medicine.[18]

> July 18th—Captain getting worse but still giving the course to steer and look after the chart.[19]

> July 21st—Captain no better but getting gradually worse. He asked for hot cloths to be put on his stomach so we did as he asked.[20]

Various remedies were tried over the ensuing days: blistering fluid, bitter tincture, linseed poultices, Seidlitz powder and brandy, bicarbonate of soda, weak tea and mutton soup. The crew carried on with their routine duties under the fine sailing conditions of a Pacific Northwest summer. There is no indication from the logbook entries as to whether or not they were apprised of the captain's worsening condition, but no doubt his lack of appearance on deck led to questions and concerns.

On August 7, Flattery Rocks were sighted eight miles distant, as the *Robert Kerr* neared the entrance to Juan de Fuca Strait. A day later, John Richardson noted the sighting of Destruction Island and the appearance of two steamers, one heading north, the other south. He added, "Captain getting worse, told me there had been nothing pass through him for three days. His voice is nearly gone."[21]

On August 10, the following entry was recorded: "At 9:15

a.m. the Captain died. Everything has been done for him that could have been done, according to his own instructions. Captain was conscious to the last, spoke for 5–6 minutes before he died, and asked for a drink of water. To the best of my belief, his complaint was dropsy and inflammation of the kidneys. — John Richardson, First Mate"[22]

The death of Captain Edwards was doubly tragic, as the *Robert Kerr* was within short days' sailing distance of Victoria. Joe and his crewmates were called aft amidst heavy squalls and drizzle to view the body of their captain before it was sewn up in canvas. He was then buried at sea according to naval tradition. John Richardson read them the official logbook entry to affirm that everything had been done according to the captain's own instructions. For the still youthful Joe, this close encounter with death must have left a lasting impression.

With John Richardson taking over the captain's duties as the *Robert Kerr* neared landfall, his logbook entries became sketchy and intermittent. On the afternoon of August 15, a pilot boat came alongside, and by four o'clock, under a light breeze, the *Robert Kerr* passed Clallam Bay. By eight in the evening, they passed Pillar Point, and at long last, the *Robert Kerr* dropped anchor in the shallows of Royal Roads, offshore from Esquimalt Harbour.[23]

Having long been used as a Hudson's Bay Company anchorage, Esquimalt now also served as the Pacific headquarters of the British Naval Fleet. On August 23, the tugboat *Alexander* hove to and towed the *Robert Kerr* into Victoria Harbour. The crew was employed mooring the ship and clearing up decks. At this point, a gap in logbook entries suggests that the crewmen were given some shore leave—a welcome diversion for Joe from the grim realities of recent weeks.

At 10:40 on the morning of September 6, the *Robert Kerr* was towed by the steam tug *Pilot* out of Royal Roads "on a voyage to Burrard's Inlet." The logbook entries continued in a different hand from John Richardson's: "After leaving the harbour we ran into a fog bank and it remained very thick until 12:50 p.m., when the ship grounded on San Juan Island. At the time of the ship striking there was a good lookout being kept and nothing was seen until within a very few yards."

All hands were called on deck immediately as the ship's movement came to a halt with a terrible crunch. Additional tow ropes were thrown to the steamer *Pilot*, and the *Robert Kerr* quickly came off the rocks. It was clear that the ship was damaged and taking on water, but not to such an extent as would warrant evacuation. "We therefore proceed towards our destination."[24]

Under continuous tow by the steam tug, the *Robert Kerr* made the crossing of Georgia Strait uneventfully. By 8:30 p.m., the Active Pass light was noted abeam, by 7:45 a.m., Passage Island. At half-past ten on the morning of September 7, the *Robert Kerr* came to anchor off Hastings Sawmill in eighteen fathoms of water.[25] For Joe and his crewmates, it was the culmination of an epic voyage from the muddy Mersey and storm-tossed Atlantic, through the blue water tropics, to the forested mountainsides and mist-shrouded islands of the Pacific Northwest Coast. Nearly a year had elapsed since they left Liverpool.

Inspections of the ship quickly ensued and the *Robert Kerr* was found to be taking on water at the rate of 3¾ inches per hour.[26] A windmill pump was employed to keep the leakage to a manageable level. While awaiting further instructions, the crew was kept busy washing the decks, attending to the pump and preparing to discharge the stone ballast. A few days later, a

Burrards Inlet B.C.

HOUR	K.	F.	COURSES	WINDS	Lee Way	REMARKS
1885 Tuesday 29th Sept						Wind and Weather as yesterday. Crew attending Pumps. Forbes & Fletcher A Bs off duty sick. Anchor light hung out and watch set *WP*
Wednesday 30th						Light variable airs and rain throughout. Crew attending Pumps Forbes AB discharged from the ship. Fletcher returned to duty. Anchor light hung out & watch set *WP*
Thursday 1st Oct						Pleasant breeze from the Westward and fine clear weather. Windmill Pump working all day. Crew employed attending Pumps and other various jobs. Anchor light & Watch set *WP*
Friday 2nd						First part Calm & thick fog. Middle and latter parts calm and clear. Crew employed attending Pumps. Anchor light hung out & watch set *WP*
Saturday 3rd						This day commences Calm with a thick fog. Middle and latter parts Calm and fine clear weather. Crew employed attending Pumps, Anchor light hung out and watch set *WP*

Course	Dist.	Dif. Lat.	Dep.	Lat. by Acct. BAROMETER	Lat. by Ob. SIN.	Dif. Lon. THERMOMETER	Lon by Acct	Lon by Ob
				Dist. per log.		Variation.		

ON THE LOOK-OUT.		NAMES	SIDE LIGHTS EXHIBITED
Sunday 4th		First part Calm & thick fog. Middle and part pleasant breeze from the Westward and fine clear weather. Windmill Pump working. Main Pump attended to. Anchor light hung out and Watch set *WP*	

Joe's discharge from service is recorded on Wednesday, September 30, 1885, in the Robert Kerr logbook. (CVA, AM35) diver was dispatched to make a thorough survey of damage to the ship's hull.

His report was not encouraging. The forefoot of the *Robert Kerr* was completely destroyed in the grounding, along with eight to ten feet of the main keel and shoe. Wooden planking on the stem and keel had been driven inward and crushed to shreds, with the outer edges projecting on either side of the ship. The metal plate at the junction of the stem and keel on the starboard side was lodged among the crushed planks. The portside plate was entirely gone. In summing up his report, the diver stated flatly, "The vessel is injured to such an extent that it is entirely beyond the limit of submarine repair."[27]

Simply put, Joe and the men of the *Robert Kerr* were shipwrecked in Granville, as the small Burrard Inlet community was then known. Several more days went by, during which the crew took turns at the wearying job of manning the pumps and trimming ballast. Complaints arose as time wore on and there appeared to be no decision forthcoming on the ship's fate. A doctor was called on board to diagnose an "ailing" William Anderson and another crewman by the name of Steward William Miller, but quickly determined that there was nothing wrong with either man. Joe booked off sick on September 25 and received a prescription. Perhaps this sealed his decision to come ashore, for on a rainy September 30, 1885, Fortes AB, was officially discharged from service aboard the *Robert Kerr*.[28]

CHAPTER 4

Odd Job Man

Vancouver, or Granville as it was then known, bore little resemblance in 1885 to the great metropolis it was destined to become, but signs of impending expansion were clearly visible. Hotels, saloons and mercantile stores lined the mud-laden Water and Carrall streets, and a constant pounding of hammers could be heard through the smoky haze of clearing fires. At the eastern edge of town, Hastings Mill bustled with industry; ancient-growth trunks of cedar and Douglas fir lay waiting to be cut into board lengths by massive circular saws. Regularly scheduled steamers tied up dockside to discharge passengers and freight, while tall ships lay at anchor up and down Burrard Inlet.

Isaac Johns, customs officer and harbour master of Granville, paid Joe his wages, in accordance with the Hudson's Bay Company. With cash in his pocket, Joe's next stop was Hastings Mill Store. The landmark establishment had been constructed around 1865 to service Mill employees. Store manager Calvert Simson had become unofficially known as the town's welcoming ambassador—the man to approach for any new arrival in need of information and advice.[1] The shelves of the Hastings Mill Store were well stocked. Joe would have been able to replenish worn shirts and trousers, as well as obtain a good supply of fresh and tinned foods, a lantern, matches, kerosene and just about anything else that a pioneering individual might require.

An October 15 entry in the *Robert Kerr* logbook notes that eight former crewmen were employed for half a day transferring the ship's remaining stores and sails to a steamer bound for Victoria.[2] As Joe makes reference to a brief return to Victoria shortly after his arrival in Granville,[3] he might have chosen to travel aboard the steamer. Finding the city devoid of employment possibilities, however, he quickly returned to the frontier community, which clearly had made an impression on him.

It is difficult to determine at what point Joe decided to drop regular usage of the name of "Seraphim" (or "Serafim" as he spelled it) among his peers.[4] The word Seraphim, originating from Hebrew, is the plural version of the word "Seraph." The Seraphim are a high ranking class of celestial beings, which were first mentioned in the Old Testament. In later periods, the Seraphim came to be recognized as the highest order of the Christian angelic hierarchy.[5] Evidently, a name that conjured up images of gentle, white-winged angels with glowing halos did not serve Seraphim Fortes well in certain circles. Ashore in Granville, he simply became known as "Joe."

Joe found his first job at Hastings Mill, stacking lumber. In

The "injured" Robert Kerr at anchor in Burrard Inlet, 1886. (CVA, WAT P30)

1885, Granville was a rather seedy town, full of rough and tumble characters who had seen their share of buck-sawing through tree trunks and sleeping on hard floors. One such individual tried to bully Joe in the early days of his employment, causing the young Trinidadian to retort, "I'm a British sailor and you can't fool me!" This only served to antagonize his adversary further, and a fist fight was quickly organized to settle the matter once and for all. With Hastings Mill accountant Alan McCartney refereeing, the fight proceeded and Joe won easily. After that "it was all right," and Joe's reputation was firmly established as that of a man not to be trifled with.[6]

A variety of odd jobs fortuitously came Joe's way. He worked aboard the merchant steam tug *Etta White* owned by Captain

Henry Smith. The *Etta* was based out of Moodyville Sawmill, on the north shore of Burrard Inlet. The *Robert Kerr* continued to play a role in Joe's life, as Captain William Soule, stevedore of Hastings Mill, had recently purchased the old wreck, made enough repairs to keep it afloat and appointed Joe as night watchman. This arrangement enabled Joe to save precious dollars in accommodation costs. Employment opportunities were never lacking, for, by early 1886, boom times had arrived. An unbroken line of Canadian Pacific Railway track between Montreal and the headwaters of Burrard Inlet, at nearby Port Moody, was complete. With the extension of the line to Vancouver well underway, settlers were arriving in ever-increasing numbers. Hotels and saloons sprouted along the Water Street corridor to meet the steady demand.

The Sunnyside Hotel, with its central location at the juncture of Water and Carrall streets, was among the more popular accommodation choices. Proprietor Harry Hemlow had recently arranged for an addition to the hotel, effectively doubling his number of rooms. The addition was built atop pilings, driven deep into the bedrock of the Burrard Inlet shoreline. At high tide, Sunnyside guests could virtually fish from their hotel room windows. Advertisements in the *Vancouver Daily Advertiser* boasted of "The Sunnyside Hotel—First Class in Every Respect."[7] In need of a porter and shoeblack for his growing clientele, Harry Hemlow gave Joe his first steady employment in the community. Joe had to swallow a certain degree of pride to take on the role of shoeblack—widely considered to be among the lowliest, most menial of jobs. It meant a workday bent over boots and shoes so thickly caked with mud and manure that they would need chiselling prior to polishing. The aptly named Water Street was just that—a thoroughfare where bog land and skunk cabbage kept company with express wagons and carriages.

Despite the drudgery of life doing odd jobs, Joe had the opportunity to witness history-making events unfolding all around him, as well as occasionally to fraternize with Sunnyside elite patrons. Hotel resident Lauchlan Hamilton no doubt shared many a story after his long days of tramping the backwoods, meticulously surveying a vast street network. The illustrious William Cornelius Van Horne, general manager and vice-president of the Canadian Pacific Railway, had arrived in town to oversee final stages of the line's completion. Determined to have a more dignified-sounding name for his railway's western terminus, Van Horne recommended that "Granville" be exchanged for "Vancouver—a name worthy of a city destined to become great."[8]

The next step was to achieve incorporation. On February 15, 1886, Joe's former boss, Hastings Mill manager Richard Alexander, presented a petition to the provincial legislature bearing 125 signatures—about one-fourth of Granville's male population. On April 2, 1886, a bill officially incorporating the City of Vancouver was passed in the provincial legislature, and four days later, Lieutenant Governor Clement Francis Cornwall signed it into law.

Work was progressing steadily on the CPR. Prospects for the oncoming railway attracted a bevy of real estate speculators to Vancouver, Scotsman Malcolm Alexander MacLean and Manitoba MP Arthur Wellington Ross among them. MacLean was elected first mayor of Vancouver on May 3. He made his victory speech from the balcony of the Sunnyside, to rousing cheers. Arthur Ross became extensively involved with city planning. His proposal to set aside the vast western peninsula known as the "Military Reserve" for Vancouver's first park (later to be named in honour of reigning Governor General Lord Stanley) would soon become a reality.

Vancouver was certainly no Liverpool, and if Joe had expected to find a public bathhouse akin to that which graced his beloved St. George's Pier Head, he would have been sorely disappointed. If one wanted to enjoy a swim in Vancouver, it meant treading carefully amongst the barnacle-encrusted boulders along the Burrard Inlet shoreline or slogging through the tidal mudflats of False Creek. Both waterways were sheltered from the powerful storms and strong waves—safe havens for seaweed, shells, crustaceans and swimmers—but were relatively devoid of any sizeable patch of soft sand. Joe and his friends made the best of it, grabbing the opportunity for a refreshing dip whenever time allowed, for the days of May and June 1886, were hotter and sunnier than any that the population could recall.

CHAPTER 5

Inferno and Renewal

June 13, 1886, dawned bright and sunny in Vancouver—the latest in a six-week unbroken stretch of unseasonably hot days. It being Sunday, Joe attended morning Catholic mass conducted by Father Patrick Fay in Blair's Hall, a small room at the rear of the Terminus Saloon on Water Street. Saloons, as usual, were doing a brisk business with most of the city's loggers and clearing crews taking the Sabbath day off to beat the heat with a tall drink.

An enormous pile of downed timbers and undergrowth flanked the southern edge of town. In their lust for productivity and profit, loggers had adopted an ingenious method of harvesting the centuries-old trees with the least degree of effort. Younger trees with narrower trucks were only partially axed through. The older giants would then be sawn strategically, so that their great weight would bring down every partially cut tree in their path as they crashed to the forest floor. It was a wonderfully inventive system by all accounts, the one drawback being that there were simply not enough oxen to haul the raw logs to the mill in timely fashion. It would take days, often weeks, before the giant trunks were stripped of their branches and transported via skid road to the waterfront. Stumps, unusable branches, roots and any other obtrusive remains were eventually burned or dynamited.

Clearing-fires were a way of life in Vancouver. Rapidly changing weather systems were not. About mid-morning June 13, not far from the shoreline of False Creek, a small company of men were struggling to regain control of a clearing fire that had roared to life with the help of a rogue wind. The men watched helplessly as flaming pieces of debris soared beyond reach of their water buckets and sailed off into the bone-dry mountain of deadfall.

Shortly after lunchtime, a thick pall of smoke began to envelop Vancouver. The first curious souls who ventured outside quickly realized that a monstrous fire was bearing down on the city. Cries of alarm rang through the streets. Joe and the Sunnyside managers, Harry Hemlow and Captain Jackman, ran from room to room, pounding on doors and shouting for guests to get out. MP Arthur Ross, together with his wife Jessie and eight-year-old son Donald, had taken up residence at the Sunnyside in early January. With Ross nowhere in sight, Joe took it upon himself to look after Jessie and young Donald.[1] As fire raged down the plank boardwalks of Water Street, there were two options for escape: outrunning the flames eastward or plunging into the waters of Burrard Inlet. While we do not have full details of the Ross family's experience, it appears that Joe shepherded them to the water and into one of the many rescue craft converging at the shoreline. Joe and Harry Hemlow themselves barely escaped with their lives, pushing off from the rear of the Sunnyside in an old scow. For several minutes they drifted about in searing heat before reaching Hastings Mill wharf. Badly scorched, they sought aid along with dozens of other victims.[2] Pain relief was haphazard amidst the confusion. Dr. William McGuigan quickly disbursed the small amount of opium that he had managed to rescue from his Carrall Street surgery. Calvert Simson and Emma Alexander, wife of the mill manager, improvised soothing poultices from skunk cabbage leaves and scraps of lint soaked in carbolated oil.

Joe survived the Great Vancouver Fire with no lasting physical trauma. The city itself did not fare as well. With the exception of the Regina Hotel at the extreme western edge of town, Hastings Mill, and a few structures on the outskirts, the entire downtown core was obliterated. There was no official word on casualties. Vancouver had a transient population and many of its inhabitants were strangers to one another. Twenty-one bundles of human remains were carefully wrapped in blankets and placed in a makeshift morgue at the Bridge Hotel, on the south shore of False Creek.[3] Relief efforts were quickly galvanized, and Vancouver emerged from the ashes like a phoenix, with neighbour helping neighbour and hammers pounding from daybreak to darkness. One can well imagine Joe throwing himself into the task of helping to rebuild. Within short weeks, new shops and saloons and hotels lined Water Street once again. Strict new fire regulations were drawn up and Joe would have been amongst the excited onlookers on August 3, 1886, when the city's first fire engine arrived from Ontario. Mayor MacLean drew laughter from the crowd as he good-naturedly received a ceremonial soaking of Burrard Inlet seawater as it gushed from the volunteer fire crew's canvas hosepipe.[4]

The Sunnyside Hotel was reconstructed, although there is no further record of Joe's employment there, and his activities for the first year or two after the fire remain somewhat of a mystery. In conversation with *Vancouver Daily News-Advertiser* columnist Noel Robinson several years later, Joe recollected that "me and the first city engineer Vancouver ever had, surveyed up the North Arm and Indian River, looking for clay to start a brickyard." He proudly added, "I struggled around in those early days, but I was always hired by the best people in the city."[5] In the wake of the Great Fire, demand for brick construction had surged. Among a long list of stringent new fire bylaws published on page one of the *Vancouver News* for July 24, 1886, was a clause requiring that ash from woodstoves and fireplaces be "contained in a brick or stone depository." Another clause read, "Every chimney or flue shall be built of brick or stone four inches in thickness, and shall be so constructed so as to admit of its being brushed and cleaned."[6] There are no records to confirm the success or failure of Joe's new venture, but with no permanent place of employment, he had clearly gone back to his old practice of obtaining work wherever he could find it.

Ground-breaking events continued to occur in Vancouver. One can well surmise that Joe stood amongst the transfixed crowd when the glistening, flower-bedecked Engine 374 pulled the first transcontinental passenger train into Vancouver on May 23, 1887. The *Vancouver Daily News-Advertiser* painted a vivid picture of the historic arrival:

OCEAN TO OCEAN—Before the train arrived, the crowd became very dense, men women and children to the number of fully two thousand were mixed up together, talking and laughing and discussing the great event of the day. At 12.45 while all were straining their eyes eastward, the loud whistle of the engine was heard, "here she comes! here she comes!" was heard on all sides and at the same time a rush for the platform was made by those on the banks above. A minute later amidst the cheers of the people, ringing of bells and the shrill cry of the locomotive whistle, the FIRST THROUGH PASSENGER TRAIN entered the station and pulled up in Vancouver.[7]

A key term in British Columbia joining Confederation was "the construction of a railway, from the Pacific towards the Rocky Mountains and from such a point as may be selected, east of the Rocky Mountains toward the Pacific, to connect the seaboard of B.C. with the railway system of Canada."[8] The arrival of the CPR was a landmark day for Vancouverites and Canadians everywhere: the long-awaited culmination of years of planning, political infighting, back-breaking labour, heartbreak and triumph.

CHAPTER 6

The Perfect Place

W hile chatting with reporters at a 1910 civic reception, Joe gave a vivid account of milestone events in his life. He recalled that he arrived in Granville in 1883 and "discovered English Bay beach on May 28 of that year"[1]—but to what year was he referring? As we know from the *Robert Kerr* logbook, Joe disembarked in Granville on September 30, 1885. Unfortunately, we must take his recollections of dates with a generous grain of salt. Owing to various factors, 1887 would be the likely year that Joe found English Bay, and with it, his true life's calling.

Joe's landmark day began simply enough with another of his ongoing string of post-fire odd jobs—providing a rowboat ride.

A logger, Simon Fraser (not the famous explorer), had asked Joe
to convey belongings and groceries from the Royal City Planing
Mills on False Creek to his small logging camp near Jerry's Cove,
now Jericho Beach. After completing the task and pocketing his
wages, Joe decided to take advantage of the long daylight hours
to explore. He rowed back across the wide expanse of water
known as English Bay, and followed the shoreline north toward
the forested peninsula that had been designated "Military Reserve," later to be known as Stanley Park. En route, he noticed
a small area of beach glistening remarkably in the afternoon sun.
Curious, he rowed to shore for a closer look. The beach was covered with tiny white crystals, sparkling amidst patches of something that actually could be described as sand. There were the
usual boulders and brush protruding up and down the shoreline,
but Joe quickly realized that he had found something unique—
"the very place for a boy's swimming beach!"[2]

The next day, Joe excitedly described his find to three of his
friends—Charlie Tilley, Arthur Jones and Hugo Ross. Eleven-
year-old Hugo had rejoined his parents, Arthur and Jessie Ross,
and younger brother Donald the previous summer, after attending boarding school in Manitoba. Joe had rescued Hugo when
the boy got into trouble during a swim in the murky backwaters
of False Creek. Ever since then, Hugo had become Joe's doting
companion. In a time when there was a great social divide between the upper and the labouring classes, MP Arthur Ross,
man of high society, was indebted to Joe for saving the lives of
his wife and both sons. This special relationship would pay div-
idends for Joe in weeks to come.

Everyone agreed that a more thorough inspection of Joe's discovery was in order. It was a lengthy row for the four of them
from Andy Linton's boat rental dock at the foot of Carrall Street,

and a hard pull against the swirling currents of the narrows, but eventually they rounded the westernmost point of the Military Reserve and came within sight of the beach. Joe's companions were amazed. Nowhere in Vancouver had they found anything quite like this! Centuries of pounding waves, head on and unbroken from the wide sweep of English Bay, had created a small paradise of sandy beach and quartz crystals. The young men were delighted as they came up on shore and lost no time in "officially taking possession of this stretch of shore as their own personal swimming beach."[3]

In reality, this region had been visited more than once before. English Bay, as the name implies, is steeped in British heritage and influence. Moreover, Squamish, Musqueam and Tsleil-Waututh natives had plied its waters for centuries. Despite much-debated speculation that Sir Francis Drake passed through during a top secret 1579 voyage in search of the Northwest Passage,[4] José Maria Narváez of Spain is credited with being the first European to explore the bay in 1791. Captain George Vancouver arrived a year later, unexpectedly encountering Spanish explorers Galiano and Valdés, who were also charting the region. Captain George Richards of the British survey ship H.M.S. *Plumper* is credited with adopting the names of English Bay and Spanish Banks,[5] likely in a nod to the cooperative relationship between Captain Vancouver and his Spanish counterparts. Captain Richards sailed further into English Bay in 1859, exploring a waterway which branched eastward from its innermost reaches. The name "False Creek" was aptly bestowed when the waterway was found to be an inlet rather than a navigable passage.

The Squamish knew Joe's "perfect place" as "Eeyulshun ("good footing"). Another nearby stretch of sand, today's Sunset Beach, was called Ee'eeyulshun ("little good footing").[6] Eeyulshun was a favourite summer camping ground, where families would set up their *kliskis* (shelters), pick berries, fish and dig for clams. A young August Jack Khatsahlano and his Squamish family paddled regularly offshore as they made seasonal journeys between their thickly forested home at Chaythoos, near Prospect Point, and the waterfowl-rich marshlands of False Creek. John Morton, one of Vancouver's earliest pioneers, recalled pulling up here years earlier with a native guide. A rough trail led through the still largely virgin West End forest, thick with salal and salmonberry. Joe and his friends were soon to make good use of the trail, finding it preferable to making the arduous row around the Military Reserve.

Before long, word of the pristine beach filtered through the city and a steadily growing entourage joined the afternoon treks to English Bay. It was a welcome opportunity to escape the ever-present stench of smoke from the clearing fires and fill one's lungs with fresh sea air. Joe could see that the rough trail through the wilderness took a toll on many of his companions. Toddlers struggled to keep up, mothers hauled perambulators over fallen logs, older children barged ahead in their eagerness, necessitating frequent stops to regroup. It was clear that the route needed improvement—ideally a wide, well-graded road. Joe decided that the best man to approach with this proposal would be none other than the mayor himself.

Mayor Malcolm MacLean, into the second spring of his two-year term in office, was the quintessential "people's mayor." He had been a rallying force in the wake of the Great Fire and had numerous items on his agenda with the arrival of the CPR, but he took time out to hear Joe's request for a road. Joe had a special place in the mayor's heart. Years earlier, Malcolm MacLean and Arthur Ross had married sisters Margaret and Jessie Cattanach.

Joe had saved the lives of MacLean's in-laws—the wife and two sons of his good friend and colleague Arthur Ross. The mayor happily assented, in principle, to the proposed construction of a road to English Bay beach.

CHAPTER 7

Bartender Standards

By the spring of 1888, Joe was working as a bartender at the Bodega Saloon, located at 21 Carrall Street. While this meant an abrupt departure from his Good Templar principles, the position of bartender was a big step up the social ladder for Joe. He became an expert at preparing cocktails and would proudly reminisce in years to come that "the fus' John Collins I ever mixed was fo' George Keefer, the C.P.R. engineer, who said it was jus' fine!"[1] Typical bartenders of the era were popular "gentlemen," bright, well-dressed and well-paid. At the Bodega, a schooner of beer sold for five cents, and whiskeys were two for a quarter.[2] Fruit juices and soda water completed the menu for the benefit of teetotallers and underage patrons. Young Gertrude

Coughtry, whose father owned a shop across the alley from the Bodega, often dropped by after school to enjoy a lemonade especially prepared for her by Joe.[3]

Now in a position of trust, Joe made daily visits to the private banking company of Casement and Creery with the bar's proceeds. Business was brisk, but perhaps could have been more lucrative if Joe had not discouraged Bodega patrons from drinking too liberally—much to the consternation of his boss, Alexander MacPherson.

"Don' you think youse had enough now?" Joe could often be heard admonishing some surprised patron. "Why don' you git home to de wife and kiddies?"

Joe also did his best to help out in the community. When Al Larwill sought volunteers to help clear a three-acre space of land on Cambie Street for Vancouver's first sports field, Joe rose to the task. Trees and stumps had been removed, but the area was still thick with brush and badly in need of levelling. It was backbreaking work to clear such a large area with little more than pickaxes and shovels. One-armed city jailer John Clough brought in a few shackled prisoners for added manpower. After several hours of swinging a pickaxe, Joe could be seen hurrying back to the Bodega from Cambie Street to scrub his hands and fingernails to bartender standards. The first cricket match at the Cambie Street Grounds took place on Dominion Day of 1888, between Vancouver and Victoria.

By now, Joe was beginning to establish a local reputation. On August 31, 1888, the following report appeared in the *Vancouver Daily News-Advertiser*:

A gloom seemed to pervade the city yesterday, especially that part lying around Carrall Street. Men went about with a sad look on their faces, dogs wore a dejected air, and even the rats seemed to feel the general depression. The cause of the universal sadness was the fact that Mr. Joseph Fortz, alias Joe, the popular bartender of the Bodega Saloon, was suffering from indisposition. He looked quite pale as he sat in a chair thoughtfully placed for him in Tattersall's stables and mused on the mutability of human affairs. All the leading physicians were in attendance and hourly bulletins were issued. Up to the time of writing, Joe, although not quite himself, was in a fair way of recovery and probably by this time as light-hearted as ever.[4]

Another report followed the next day: "The announcement that Mr. Joseph Fortz has fully recovered his spirits and his colour will cause a ripple of pleasure in every circle of society. The rats on Carrall Street whisked their tails last night with their accustomed cheerfulness and all nature wore a smiling aspect."[5] There is no record as to the cause of Joe's affliction, although it appears that he was in genuinely good medical hands.

Eeyulshun, more frequently known as English Bay or First Beach, steadily grew in popularity as Vancouver's population swelled. If the Great Fire produced one advantage, it was that it had cut a wide swath across the debris-strewn landscape, enabling clearing crews to forge ahead with new roads and construction. Burrard Street was becoming a reality, as was Georgia. From this intersection, a sinuous trail meandered in the direction of English Bay. At the future right-of-way for Denman Street, it would eventually meet a three-foot-wide plank sidewalk—not quite the spacious roadway agreed upon by Mayor MacLean, but a welcome relief from the marshland underfoot.

Among the earliest residents of English Bay beach was a family by the name of Simpson. For the sum of fifty dollars, brothers

Zachary and William Simpson purchased a logger's shack and pigpen, which had been erected in the area some years previously. They soon built English Bay's very first bathing pavilion—a primitive shanty with a board door and a small window, where women and children could change into their bathing costumes for a small fee. However rustic, the structure was certainly preferable to hiding amidst the scratchy salmonberry and salal while disrobing.

In the fall of 1890, a sickly Mrs. Mackay and her three children moved into the logger's shack while the Simpsons travelled to eastern Canada. Annie Mackay, at age thirteen the eldest of the three children, proved to be a resourceful young lady who took it upon herself to provide for her ailing mother and siblings. Gathering up pieces of driftwood, shingles and anything else useable that happened to wash up on the beach, Annie built her own rudimentary bathing pavilion and charged five cents per person for its use. Although there would have been little demand that first winter, Annie saw a steady run of customers as days lengthened and grew warmer. She also came to appreciate the presence of Joe, who came to the beach at least once a week during his Wednesday afternoons off-duty from the Bodega. In a 1932 interview with Vancouver City Archivist Major Matthews, Annie vividly recalled her impressions:

> At first, I presume Joe came for his own enjoyment, but was so agreeable and pleasant that we began to expect and watch for his coming. Of course, he had no salary; he was just a great big black man. If anything went wrong—or if any man intruded into the woman's part, or broke the rules—there would be a great big halloo. Either some man would give him a big swift kick or "Old Joe" would come along and haul the intruder back into the man's part.[6]

The Simpson/Mackay residence and a glass house were among the few
structures at English Bay beach in 1889. (CVA, BeP4N75)

A very large boulder stood at the shoreline, about three hundred feet east of where present-day Denman Street lies. Perhaps
recalling the separate bathing facilities he had witnessed at St.
George's Pier Head, Joe designated the boulder as a boundary
between the men's and women's bathing beaches. Women and
children were limited to the beach area south of the boulder,
which allowed them the use of the bathing pavilions, while men
were limited to the north. Victorian prudishness still reigned
supreme in the late nineteenth century. A City of Vancouver
"vagrancy" bylaw drawn up in 1892 ordered that "no person
shall bathe or swim in the waters of Burrard Inlet or English
Bay within the City limits between the hours of 6 o'clock in the
forenoon and 8 o'clock in the evening without a bathing dress
covering the body from the neck to the knees."[7]

As time progressed, Joe steadily familiarized himself with
English Bay beach and its regular habitués. He came to have an

uncanny ability to anticipate trouble—perhaps an intuitive trait common among bartenders. Whether monitoring the alcohol consumption of Bodega patrons or the behaviour of certain beachgoers, Joe performed his roles to the highest of "bartender standards."

CHAPTER 8

Guardian, Teacher and Friend

W hen a worldwide economic recession drastically slowed
Vancouver's expansion through much of the 1890s, people sought escape and solace at English Bay. Joe was an imposing
figure among the beach-goers, and few were inclined to question
his authority. Mothers sent off their children with the stern
order, "Don't go away from where Joe is!"[1] Athletic young men
in one-piece woollen bathing suits followed his advice for mas-
tering the popular strokes and diving techniques of the day.
Fashionable ladies struggled diligently in the shallows, weighted
down under voluminous skirts of black satin, with straw boaters
carefully pinned into position to hold against the sea breeze. Holiday cottages, constructed of lumber floated down from the

Royal City Planing Mills of False Creek, sprang up along the shoreline in increasing numbers. Wooden walkways slanted from verandas to the water's edge. The Simpson brothers, having returned from back east, undertook to expand their fortunes with the construction of a multi-storey wood-frame bathhouse and boathouse.

As English Bay became more popular, there was a growing need for a formalized life-saving program of some kind. Lifeguards, however, were relatively rare in Joe's time. The Royal Life Saving Society had been founded in England in 1891 to combat an ever-increasing number of deaths due to drowning, but affiliates of the organization were yet to materialize in other areas of the Commonwealth. The first Canadian branch was not established until 1908, in Ontario, and a British Columbia branch finally appeared in 1911.

Life-saving methods were not widely understood, and a bizarre array of techniques, developed over centuries of experimentation, had failed to produce any formally recognized method. Cardiopulmonary resuscitation (CPR) was unknown, and though mouth-to-mouth resuscitation was starting to emerge as a reviving technique, it was not yet fully comprehended. The most widely approved resuscitative action in the later part of the nineteenth century was the "Silvester Method," invented by an English physician by the name of Henry Robert Silvester. Dr. Silvester's technique involved laying patients on their back with arms raised on either side of the head. The arms were then brought down and pressed hard against the chest. This movement, repeated sixteen times per minute, was designed to draw air into the lungs, thereby reviving the victim. The traditional remedies of a liberal dose of smelling salts or tickling the throat with a feather could also be brought into play.

With no formal assistance in place, Joe began teaching swimming technique in addition to keeping a wary eye on the swimmers at English Bay. Of the many Vancouverites who in later years would recall their experiences of being taught to swim by Joe, most would agree that his favourite mantra was "Kick yo' feet!" Child after child would gather around him, clamouring for their turn to be hoisted up by a thick handful of bathing costume, suspended horizontally in the water and commanded to kick for all they were worth. "Thas' it! You can do it! Now thas' just dandy!" However unconventional Joe's teaching methods, there is little doubt that he instilled an enthusiasm and confidence in his pupils that raised their swimming capability to new heights.

Joe made many friends in Vancouver, but he was to establish a particular bond with an African-American family by the name of Scurry. Hiram Scurry and his sons Charles and Elijah had arrived in Vancouver in the early days of 1886. Hiram's wife Martha arrived weeks later aboard the first through CPR train from Winnipeg to Port Moody with the rest of the family—Harvey, Albert and a little girl named Cassie, short for Catherine. Originally from Illinois, Martha was the daughter of a former slave who had bought her way to freedom by selling apple pies.[2]

Together with his sons, Hiram opened a barbershop and shaving parlour at the corner of Carrall and Oppenheimer streets. After losing everything in the Great Fire, the Scurrys reestablished their business on Abbott Street. Always appearing well-coiffed and clean-shaven in his photographs, Joe spent a good portion of time in the Scurry barbershop. In the summer months, Joe's life centred on his as-yet-unofficial work at English

Bay, and his bartending duties at the Bodega. But during the dark nights of winter, he enjoyed many a cheerful evening in the comfort of the Scurry parlour, chatting with the family or playing checkers with Cassie—who would take great delight in crowning her game pieces when Joe wasn't looking.[3] Like Joe, the Scurry brothers were natural athletes, and they took great pleasure in discussing the Vancouver sporting scene of the day.

Sadly for the Scurry family and for Joe, Hiram Scurry died of Bright's disease, inflammation of the kidneys, on October 23, 1895, at the age of sixty-three. Hiram's passing saw Joe take on the role of a father figure to the grief-stricken Scurrys, aiding and comforting them in their loss.

To make ends meet, Martha Scurry opened a boarding house at 228 Abbott Street, which soon became a mecca for unemployed seamen from all corners of the world. Ever generous, Martha always seemed to be able to squeeze in one more lad who was far from home and down on his luck. Many would promise remittance; seldom did it appear. "When my ship comes in, I'll remember you, Mrs. Scurry," was the oft-heard refrain, much to the annoyance of streetwise Joe, who privately scoffed at such declarations.[4] Nevertheless, Christmas at the Scurry boarding house was a sumptuous affair of plates piled high with turkey, goose and suckling pig, later to be capped off with a rousing singalong of sea shanties. Through much resourcefulness, the Scurry family, together with Joe, continued to make ends meet.

It could be argued that Vancouver's recovery from the economic doldrums of the 1890s began at a remote Yukon river on the starry night of August 16, 1896. Prospector George Carmack, his wife Kate Carmack, Skookum Jim Mason and Dawson Charlie made camp alongside Rabbit Creek, a tributary of the Klondike River in the Yukon Territory. The group panned the muddy gravel of the creek bed and soon discovered one of the greatest gold deposits ever recorded.[5]

Vancouver, along with cities up and down the Pacific Northwest Coast, became a major supply point for the gold seekers that stampeded north as word of the discovery leaked out. The ensuing Klondike gold rush became a major catalyst in drawing Vancouver out of recession and into a new era of prosperity and expansion.

It is hard to imagine a young, physically fit and unattached Joe not getting caught up in the frenzy of the stampede. By the summer of 1897, numerous retail outfitters had mushroomed in the downtown core. Starry-eyed men grabbed supplies off shelves as fast as they could be restocked. Fully-loaded steamers were departing regularly for Skagway, Alaska. However tempting it may have been to pull up stakes and join the throngs heading north, Joe remained behind. His close attachment to the Scurry family undoubtedly played a role in his decision.

Martha Scurry ran her burgeoning business with a fierce determination to keep her family housed and well fed. Joe took up residence, no doubt as a shoulder for Martha to lean upon as well as a tenant. Martha was a handsome woman and while there was no romantic attachment, he would have been reluctant to leave her to manage alone amidst an occasionally dubious clientele.

Other factors kept Joe from heeding the Klondike call. By now an experienced bartender, he had secured a position at the prestigious Alhambra Hotel, one of the city's first structures to be built of brick following the Great Fire. Business thrived at the Alhambra, thanks to an endless stream of stampeders. Every room featured a fireplace—a welcome luxury, for which guests were more than happy to lay down the dollar-per-night charge.

And, of course, Joe was still needed, and increasingly *expected*,

Martha Scurry—Joe's friend and confidant,
1899. (COURTESY HOWARD FAMILY)

to maintain watch at English Bay. Many Klondike-bound individuals, conscious of the fact that they were heading into remote and frigid realms, seized the opportunity for one last carefree day on a sunny beach. The June 8, 1898, edition of the Victoria *Daily Colonist* reported one gentleman's misadventures: "J. Mc-Cook, the newly appointed United States consul for Dawson City, was overcome with heart failure while bathing in English Bay and rescued from certain death by a colored man named Joe Fortes, after he had disappeared for the third time. Fortes dived under his body and brought him up to the surface and resuscitated him." The grateful McCook recommended that Joe be awarded a medal from the Royal Humane Society.[6]

Now into his thirties and beginning to receive recognition, Joe was maturing and settling. He had steady employment, responsibility, respect and a family that he could call his own. While others saw fortunes made and lost in the Klondike, Joe had found his own form of "gold."

CHAPTER 9

The Angel and the Pirates

Most significant in his decision not to join the stampede north was Joe's dedication to his Catholic faith. One of his most treasured possessions was a copy of Thomas à Kempis' *Imitation of Christ*. Long a staple of Catholic devotions, the book advocated the virtues of a simple and frugal lifestyle:

> Four Things That Bring Great Peace:
> Always strive, my son, to do another's will rather than your own.
> Always choose to have less rather than more.
> Always seek the lowest place and be submissive in all things.
> Always desire and pray that God's will be entirely fulfilled in you.
> The man who accomplishes all this advances toward peace and rest.[1]

What use would a wealth of gold be to Joe when he believed in passages such as these? When all of his needs and wants were so amply furnished in Vancouver?

From his earliest days in Vancouver, Joe had attended Catholic services wherever he could find them. The little back room known as Blair's Hall, where Father Patrick Fay had conducted his services, was nothing but a memory after the Great Fire, and a proper church had since been erected. It is said that when Father Fay was asked where he and his parishioners would like their new church to be located, he pointed to the tallest tree that he could see from the waterfront. "We choose the section surrounding the base of that tree!"[2]

The wooden Our Lady of the Church of the Holy Rosary that arose was Joe's house of worship for several years. By the late 1890s, however, it was clear that a much larger facility would be required to accommodate the city's ever-growing Catholic population. On July 16, 1899, a crowd of over one thousand gathered to witness a monumental event at Richards and Dunsmuir—the ceremonial laying of a cornerstone for a new and massive Church of Our Lady of the Holy Rosary. The church, which had already been under construction for several months, was to be a gathering place for Vancouver's Catholic community quite unlike anything the city had ever seen. Designed in the shape of a 218-foot-long cross by architect T.E. Julian, the building would feature Gothic-style arches, buttresses, a vaulted ceiling and stained glass windows. Its spire would be visible from ships rounding the narrows into Burrard Inlet. A total of seven bells, named after the seven sacraments, were being cast in Savoy, France. But the church's proudest feature would be its electrical pipe organ. Built by D.W. Karn and Co. in Woodstock, Ontario, the $7,500 organ featured three manuals of 61 notes each, a pedal of 30 notes and a total of 2,468 pipes.[3] Joe and his fellow parish-ioners sat transfixed during many a Sunday service, listening to the sounds of the Holy Rosary organ reverberating throughout the sanctuary.

There is no evidence that Joe wore his faith on his sleeve or attempted to preach to the unconverted among the throngs at English Bay. His lifestyle exemplified frugality and he took great pleasure in simple gestures, such as giving out handkerchiefs as prizes at church picnics. He had his own favourite seat in the church, which he occupied faithfully every Sunday.

By the turn of the century, City Council could no longer ignore the need for formalized supervision at English Bay beach. This realization was no doubt fuelled by a citizen's requisition placed before City Council on May 21, 1900, bearing a large number of signatures and requesting that Joe be given a salary in exchange for his ongoing services at the beach.[4] Joe would always recall how "the mayor (Mayor James Garden) and several of the alder-men came down and called me out of the water to give me the job."[5] On June 1, 1900, Joe became an official city employee, with a monthly salary of eighty dollars.[6] In return, he would be ex-pected to provide lifeguarding, swimming instruction and beach patrol services as a special constable.

The timing could not have been better. Only days previously on May 20, the first electric streetcar service connected Granville and Denman streets via Robson and Davie. Now that the jour-ney from downtown could be made with relative ease, hordes of beachgoers descended on English Bay.

Of course there were still the fortunate beachgoers who lived within close proximity to English Bay. Eight-year-old William

Heilbron was among a gang of young lads who enjoyed just such a privilege. The boys spent many summer days on the sands, immersing themselves in the delights of childhood imagination. They were pirates who, with driftwood swords and dirt-stained bandanas, wreaked terror up and down the Spanish Main of English Bay. One day the pirates decided that the time had come to affirm their rule with a truly daring feat. For the past several years, Bill and Zach Simpson had steadily built up a thriving rowboat and canoe rental business. Their latest and proudest addition was a twenty-five-foot steam-powered launch, which they moored on the beach well above the high tide line. A set of wooden rollers was used to trundle it down to the water.

The pirates' top-secret plan was to capture the Simpson craft and steal away onto the high seas. Stealthily they crept up, grasped the sides and stern of the boat, and proceeded to heave it to the water's edge. Before long, shouts of triumph and laughter echoed up and down the beach. The pirate crew was out in the waves, tooting the launch whistle, ringing the engine bell and bellowing orders to each other.

"Enemy craft approaching to port!" one lad, who had designated himself as "the lookout," yelled. "It's coming fast!"

"The skipper" frantically pulled the bell to signal for more speed. "Chief Engineer" William froze in fear, before closing down the throttle. Special Constable Joe Fortes was drawing up alongside in one of the Simpsons' fastest rowboats. Before long, the pirates were back on shore, arranged in line by rank. Fun and games forgotten, they faced an ominous-looking Joe. Were they to be arrested? Thrown in jail for thievery? After all, Joe now had the power to make arrests!

One by one, the pirates received a sound spanking. Not a word of their delinquency was reported to their parents. No names were recorded. No record was filed. In recalling the piracy incident of 1900 in later years, William Heilbron would admit that Joe Fortes was "the greatest child psychologist I have ever known."[7] Perhaps Joe was only recalling a certain misdemeanour on a long-ago night in Liverpool.

CHAPTER 10

Triumphs and Tribulations

Throughout the years Joe became well known for saving the lives of many Vancouver children and adults. The newspapers of the day, in particular the *Vancouver Daily Province*, gave over many column inches to describing Joe's feats. In fact, they often elevated Joe to hero status amongst the citizens of Vancouver:

RESCUED FROM DEATH
Joe Fortes, Swimming Master, Saves a Little Boy

Joe Fortes, lately appointed swimming instructor at English Bay by order of the city council, has already earned his salary. Yesterday afternoon, about 4:30 o'clock, the 5-year-old son of Mrs. A. Waddell was playing at the beach. He had taken off his boots and stockings and managing to elude observation, had succeeded in wading some yards from shore. While playing in the water, he attracted the attention of two large dogs, which in a spirit of playfulness, attempted and finally succeeded in knocking the boy down. His cries were heard by Joe Fortes and although the youngster had been submerged for some time, it is due to Joe's promptitude that he was finally restored safe and sound to his parents.

— *Vancouver Daily Province*, June 16, 1900[1]

SHOULD HAVE THE MEDAL
Joe Fortes' Bravery Saves Man and Wife
From a Watery Grave

Joe Fortes saved two more lives last night at English Bay. The wind was blowing very stiff from the westward and a man and his wife were in a sailboat out in the Gulf. They were seen sailing in all right enough just about dusk, when Joe retired to his house. Not long afterwards, the whole place was roused by shrieks and cries for help. The boat had capsized and the people were struggling for their lives in the water. Without waiting to even strip, Joe rushed in and swimming out, managed to rescue both.

— *Vancouver Daily Province*, August 25, 1900[2]

While Joe enjoyed his growing celebrity reputation, the 1900 swimming season would prove to be far from smooth sailing. In the heat of August, a record-breaking salmon run began making its arduous return journey from the Pacific Ocean depths to interior spawning grounds. As twilight descended each evening, dozens of fishing boats plied the waters off Spanish Banks, their navigation lights aglow like tiny, roving beacons. Employees of the English Bay Cannery (established since 1898 at the foot of Trutch Street on the Bay's southern shore) worked feverishly to keep up with processing the bonanza of fish. All too soon, supply exceeded capacity. Angry fishermen were often compelled to dump large quantities of their catch overboard, upon learning that the day's established quota was far lower than anticipated. For several weeks, with every incoming tide, there came a profusion of discarded, dead salmon.

> Dead salmon lay on the shore in thousands. The ebb and flow of each tide rolled them backwards and forwards on the sands. Strolling on the sands of English Bay was "dangerous", especially in the twilight, for a decaying fish, half buried in the sand, was unnoticeable until, by a slipping step, it was detected; at other times, a foot trod upon one, and the decaying fish stuck to the boot; the smell was extremely objectionable, could not be easily removed, and it was impossible to go home by street car until it had. For [a] time, bathing was almost stopped entirely. A floating carcass, badly decayed after a week in the water, would bump a swimmer's chin, or a swimming stroke would break it in two.[3]

Joe's fish tribulations would soon be followed by more unpleasantness. There was the occasional individual who took exception to his employment:

> I think this [Joe Fortes' employment] is most absurd, and as a taxpayer, I must protest against anything of the kind being done. If the residents of English Bay want Mr. Fortes, let them have him, and also pay for him, as they should have done from the start. It would be far more to their interests if the money that was spent on that man had been spent on our streets instead of paying a man to look after the public.
>
> Ratepayer, *Vancouver Daily News-Advertiser*,
> October 13, 1900[4]

I would not allow a coloured man or any other man to learn my girls to swim. It's a sight you would not see at any of the watering places I have been, such as Kingstown, Newcastle, Bundoran,

Hollywood, Brighton and Bangor. In fact, the men would not be allowed within a stone's throw of where the women bathed, much less having a swimming instructor as a man amongst them!

Ratepayer, Vancouver Daily News-Advertiser,
October 17, 1900[5]

At least two readers came to Joe's defence:

I, as another ratepayer and also one who has visited "watering places" (perhaps not for such a period of time as your worthy correspondent) most emphatically assert that men are appointed and paid at public expense to look after matters of such moment to the whole community. . . . I further trust that our city fathers will see their way clear to retain the services of one who has proved himself faithful and efficient when duty called.

Another Ratepayer, Vancouver Daily News-Advertiser,
October 20, 1900[6]

Mr. Joseph Fortes, who has more than paid for the few dollars he has received this summer while employed as swimming instructor, etc., at the bathing beach, English Bay, by saving quite a number of lives which are to-day to his credit on the records of the city. The amount of Fortes' wages that Ratepayer pays, if the truth were known, would not buy him a five cent glass of pop each year.

Another Ratepayer, Vancouver Daily News-Advertiser,
October 20, 1900[7]

There is no indication that Joe read, or was made aware of these letters. In truth, he maintained watch with an eagle eye and wasted no time in clamping down on any perceived mischief on his beach. One day, not long into his official status, Special Constable Joe came across a young couple engaged in a romantic encounter. Outraged, he hauled them before a magistrate, explaining that the pair had behaved with "agglutinanted auspiciousness." The magistrate realized that Joe, no doubt hopeful of sounding scholarly and authoritative, had substituted "agglutinanted" for "agglutinated," meaning "stuck or clumped together." He burst into gales of laughter and dismissed the case.[8]

Victorian attitudes such as those described in the anti-Joe "Ratepayer" letters were slowly on the wane—as was the aging Queen Victoria herself. On January 21, 1901, an outpouring of grief consumed British colonies throughout the world at the news that Queen Victoria had died at the age of eighty-one. Joe, like other British subjects in Vancouver, would have attended one of the many memorial services held throughout the city in her honour.

Even though most citizens were in favour of Joe's employment, nevertheless, Alderman Thomas Neelands of the Vancouver City Council decided to give Joe a particularly rough ride as the 1901 summer swimming season approached. It had been resolved by the City's Police and Fire Committee to have Joe "appointed from the first day of May at a salary of $80.00 per month, subject to dismissal at any time without notice."[9] Alderman Neelands spoke out against the appointment, explaining that he felt that Joe's appointment had been secured under false pretences. According to Neelands' version of events, the public requisition for Joe's employment, which bore so many signatures, had been circulated with the understanding that every person who wrote down his or her name would be required to pay a small amount each month. Neelands pointedly claimed that when the requisition had been placed before Council, it was in the guise of a citizens' petition, the provision for financing conveniently omitted. Furthermore, Joe's appointment had been approved for three months, and then extended. Alderman Neelands' arguments came thick and fast:

If the position were once again offered to Joe, a bad precedent would be set. Joe evidently considers that he can secure a living out of the City without working for it. If he really wishes employment, give him something at which he can give the City a fair return in labour, not by spending time loafing at English Bay. English Bay is not the most dangerous place in the city, and Fortes cannot be in more than one place at a time. He would therefore stop but a small danger gap. As for Joe's special-constable status, better conduct has not prevailed at the beach than before![10]

Alderman Foreman fell in with Alderman Neelands. He pointed out that Joe's Special Constable badge should have been taken away from him at the end of last year's swimming season. This had not been done, and Joe had used it afterwards on several occasions when he should not have done so.

Despite the men's protestations, the majority of the city councillors agreed that Joe's lifeguarding skills were too invaluable to lose. It was quickly decided that his summer duties would begin on May 15, two weeks later than the date originally suggested. His off-season employment as a special constable would be at the discretion of the Police and Fire Committee.

At some unrecorded point in the early days of his city employee status, Joe took up residence in a canvas tent at the southeast corner of Davie and Denman streets. He was joining beachgoers who for several years had been helping themselves to small parcels of English Bay waterfront. A ragtag assortment of tents, driftwood lean-tos and rudimentary shacks lined the shore. Joe's tent stood atop a wooden platform, ensuring a floor that was high and dry on rainy days. The platform was long enough to hold a dining table and two chairs. Joe regularly purchased his groceries

Joe and his tent residence at English Bay, c. 1900. (CVA, PORT 1725)

and tobacco from Cheapside, a wholesale outlet run by George Wagg at 108 Water Street. On fine evenings, he could enjoy smoking his pipe and admiring the sunset from his "veranda."

By comparison, other residences in the vicinity of English Bay were far more grand. On July 23, 1901, sugar magnate Benjamin Tingley Rogers and his wife Mary hosted a gala house warming party at Gabriola, their spectacular new mansion situated by the corner of Davie and Nicola. The West End was rapidly becoming Vancouver's "blue blood" neighbourhood as more and more Vancouver business folk rose to prominence and chose to establish fine residences within a short carriage ride of the beach.

In September of that same year, Vancouver became festooned

with Union Jacks to celebrate the visit of the Duke and Duchess of Cornwall and York, later to become King George V and Queen Mary. Joe, ever proud of his British heritage, was among the welcoming crowds.

Meanwhile, Joe's status as a permanent employee continued to require City Council approval from year to year. The uncertainty was exacerbated when his nemesis Alderman Neelands was elected mayor of Vancouver in 1902. It was not until January of 1904 that City Council established a clear policy with the Vancouver Park Board over responsibility for English Bay beach. The general public quickly seized upon the clarification and circulated another petition:

> To His Worship the Mayor and Aldermen of the City of Vancouver—Gentlemen—We the undersigned citizens and ratepayers of the City of Vancouver humbly petition your honourable body to make the appointment permanent of Mr. Joseph Fortes, as city caretaker and swimming instructor at English Bay.
>
> For several years, Mr. Fortes has been in charge of the swimming beach at the Bay and during such period, has been instrumental in saving the lives of a number of people. With the young people Mr. Fortes is especially popular and more than anyone else has been instrumental in teaching the young how to swim. Mr. Fortes is a pioneer citizen and as he has always given every satisfaction as a city employee and is exceedingly qualified, WE HEREBY PETITION your honourable body to make his appointment permanent and consider the same to be a public necessity.[11]

The list of signatures that followed represented a who's who of Vancouver citizenry. H.V. Wilbur, president of the Vancouver Shipmasters Association signed, as did real estate agent Walter Graveley. Miss L. White of 923 Granville signed. Charlie Wood-

ward, owner of the brand new department store and food empo-
rium at Hastings and Abbott, signed. J. Oppenheimer scrawled
an addendum: "and 2000 others." Plumbers, blacksmiths, firemen and housewives all added their signatures to the cause. The
petition was presented before City Council on March 21, 1904,[12]
and eventually ratified by the City Finance Committee on May
6,[13] with one stalling tactic: Joe's official duties would not com-
mence until June 1, when the weather would be more conducive
to swimming. On May 31, the following article appeared in the
Vancouver Daily Province:

> City Swimming Instructor Joe Fortes, who has saved so many
> lives at English Bay that he has lost track of the number, added
> another to his list of persons rescued from the waters of English
> Bay. A boy about ten years of age, who was seized with a cramp
> caused by the coldness of the water, was pulled out by Mr. Fortes
> in the nick of time. The rescue was an overtime job, so to speak,
> as Joe happened to be at the beach at the time, although his
> official duties do not commence until tomorrow. The bathing
> beach has been largely patronized during the last week. Today,
> Mr. Fortes was duly sworn in as a special policeman at English
> Bay, in addition to his duties as swimming instructor, which will
> commence tomorrow. As the water is rather cold as yet, Mr.
> Fortes recommends children and others contemplating bathing
> not to go in before 4 o'clock.[14]

Although Joe's summer employment was now secure, his off-
season status continued to hang in the balance. Hoping to avoid
the red tape and controversy of previous years, Joe approached
former city alderman Robert Clark to act as his representative.
On October 28, Clark met with the Finance Committee to ask
if Joe could be appointed "Special Constable at English Bay for
the winter months on a reduced salary." The request was "laid
over for one week to consult with the Chief of Police."[15] On

November 8, the Secretary of Police Commissioners informed the Police and Fire Committee that Joe Fortes had been appointed Special Constable at English Bay without salary.

Once again the matter was "referred to the Finance Committee."[16] Three days later, Joe himself appeared before the Finance Committee to ask if he could be allotted a small salary. His request was "laid over for consideration."[17] On December 2, Joe appeared again and asked that "his remuneration as caretaker of the beach be fixed." It was resolved that he "be advanced twenty-five dollars on account, pending a settlement of final arrangements."[18] Finally, on December 9, 1904, the minutes of the City Finance Committee, attended by Aldermen Odlum, Stewart, McDonald and Williams, recorded that "Mr. Joe Fortes be appointed caretaker at English Bay Beach at a salary of $40.00/month. Carried."[19]

Though the ensuing years, Joe would continue to experience frustrations over his employment status, but none to compare with the runaround he was given during that fall of 1904.

CHAPTER 11

A New Home

Although a 1904 Vancouver directory lists Joe's home address as 535 Cambie, the residence of the Scurry family, he likely continued to reside in his tent during the summer months. As he was now officially expected to patrol English Bay beach on evenings throughout the year, it soon became too time-consuming and impractical for him to make the daily commute from the centre of town, especially in the bleak winter months.

Joe's problem was soon to be resolved. As English Bay grew in popularity, it became abundantly clear to City Council and the Park Board that private beachfront properties and throngs of the general public demanding beach access were a poor mix. Although completely reliant on City coffers, the Park Board devised an ambitious plan of gradually buying up all privately owned homes and businesses on the water side of Beach Avenue for conversion to public domain. The standard practice was for city firemen to oversee demolition of the structures by burning them where they stood.

Among the properties slated for demolition was a small cottage at the foot of Gilford Street. Said to be among the oldest Vancouver structures, it had recently been vacated by William Dalton and his wife, Annie, a poet. The Daltons, having arrived in Vancouver from England the previous year, enjoyed living at the beach but were in dire need of a larger abode to house their vast collection of clocks, pewter, fine china and glassware.[1] Joe examined the cottage, noted that it was structurally sound despite its age and formulated a plan. It would not be unreasonable for the cottage to be placed on skids and moved to a new location further down the waterfront—away from the area being redeveloped for public access. A plot of land at the foot of Bidwell Street ideally suited Joe's purpose. Here he could reside in comfort year-round and be virtually within shouting distance of the beach if trouble arose.

In typical fashion, Joe went straight to the top with his request, seeking approval from Mayor Fred Buscombe. Buscombe was a working-class mayor from Mount Pleasant, who undoubtedly recognized that granting the popular lifeguard his wish would not only be reasonable, but politically prudent. Within a few weeks, all the necessary paperwork was completed and Joe's new home, jackscrewed off its foundation, was transported by horsepower and skids along the three-block stretch of Beach Avenue promenade from Gilford to the foot of Bidwell Street. Although no records can be found to document this move, it is safe to assume that Joe received many offers of assistance and plenty of

Joe poses proudly with his new house, 1905.
(VPL SPECIAL COLLECTIONS, VPL 64393)

goodwill to help accomplish his endeavour. A brief note among the Finance Committee minutes for April 7, 1905, states, "Joe Fortes asking attention to accommodation at English Bay. Referred to Health Inspector."[2] Clearly the house moving was accomplished well in advance of the summer season. Joe was thrilled and proud to have a home and street address that he could truly call his own—1708 Beach Avenue.[3]

In 1905 the first official Park Board bathhouse was constructed at a cost of six thousand dollars. The imposing three-storey wooden structure at the foot of Denman Street featured a wealth of amenities: men's and ladies' changing rooms, the latest plumbing fixtures, bathing suit and towel rentals and a rooftop veranda

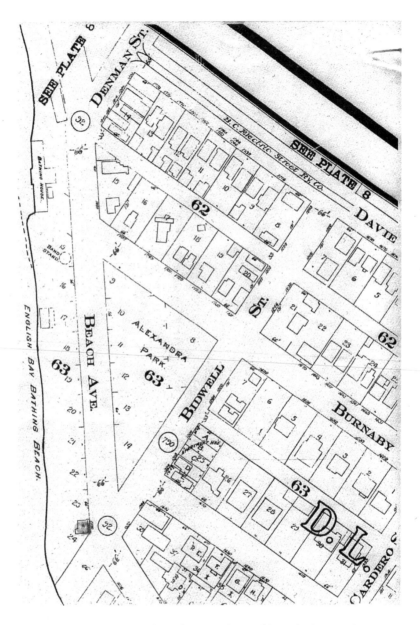

The exact location of Joe's house is discernible at the intersection of Bidwell Street and Beach Avenue on this early Vancouver fire insurance map. (CVA, GOAD'S ATLAS, MAP 342, PLATE 145)

One of few known photos which include the boundary rock, visible to the right of the 1905 Vancouver Park Board bathhouse, 1908. (CVA, BEP116)

where fastidious beachgoers could take in the glorious panorama of English Bay without the discomfort of sand between their toes. If the bathhouse had one flaw, it was its location mere footsteps from the high tide line, exposing the entire structure to potentially damaging winter storms.

The taming and refinement of English Bay beach continued at a frenetic pace. Barge loads of sand dredged from the vast deposits near Spanish Banks were pumped and spread along the length and breadth of the beach. The sand covered the remaining tiny quartz crystals that had managed to escape being pocketed by young beachcombers over the years. Joe revelled in the improvements and happily offered his professional advice on the construction of sandcastles. He knew exactly how a tunnel should be dug to connect castle gardens and where to find some pink seaweed for the flower beds. Obtrusive boulders, including the giant that had served as a boundary between male and female swimmers, were hauled away by donkey engine or buried where they sat. The policy of separate bathing areas for male and female swimmers had long been relaxed.

The exclusive Vancouver Amateur Swimming Club began meeting in June, largely composed of young gentlemen eager to test the skills they had learned over the years from Joe. Club members swam throughout the year in all weathers. Chiselled and muscular, they plied the water with the grace and agility of dolphins. Their first water polo matches were held that summer, and the first annual swimming races began from a float in front of the new bathhouse. The events drew huge crowds. There could not have been a prouder spectator than Joe, seeing his former pupils demonstrating their prowess.

English Bay beach drew an eclectic mix of young and old, wealthy and poor, local and foreign. Public mischief was rarely, if ever, a problem, but with increased crowds came the increased potential for trouble. Joe had one of his first challenging encounters on the afternoon of August 2:

FORTES PLUCK
Saved a Serious, Hysterical Riot at English Bay

About 4 o'clock on Wednesday afternoon, there came as near being a riot as ever occurred at English Bay. Mr. Josef Fortes, swimming instructor and policeman at the Bay, was in the water giving his usual afternoon instructions, when there was the sound of a row of the most serious kind in the city bathhouse. The language that was used would have made a bargee blush. Mr. Simpson, in charge of the bathhouses, sent out a cry for police, and Mr. Fortes, in his bathing suit, hurried to the spot. There, he found a man who gave his name as Wilkins in a very bad state of pugilistic intoxication. Mr. Fortes grappled with him and the man, seeing his advantage, used his boots on Mr. Fortes' bare feet. The guardian of the beach made the best of his upper muscles and got control and got the man out onto the road on Beach Avenue. He was very much in undress uniform and could not take the man to the police station. Citizens who were present say that Mr. Fortes' coolness and pluck saved a great deal of trouble, as there was a picnic party of Sunday School children from New Westminster, besides the usual crowd at the beach. Had there been a patrol box at the beach, Mr. Fortes could have locked the man up until he got dressed and then taken or sent him into custody. As it was, the man, after being sobered, got a bathing suit and went into the water. But he behaved himself after that.[4]

Publicized episodes such as this helped Joe to affirm that he was in charge and that misdemeanours of any kind would not be tolerated on "his beach." Dogs off-leash were strictly forbidden. Garbage was to be burned, buried or packed up and taken home. Vulgar language was inexcusable. Joe was the king of his domain and his castle was a little green cottage on the shore of English Bay.

CHAPTER 12

Rights and Racism

As the 1906 summer season approached, the seemingly never-ending controversy over Joe's employment arose once again. Having received notification from the city comptroller that he was officially under the jurisdiction of the Vancouver Park Board, Joe approached the board for instructions. He wanted absolute confirmation that he had been placed at English Bay as swimming instructor and special constable for three months of the year at a salary of seventy-five dollars per month, and as a special constable for the remainder of the year at forty dollars per month.

While there was no doubt as to the necessity of Joe's summertime job, park officials seemed to take particular exception to his special constable status in the off-season. They argued that the Simpson brothers, well-established with their boathouse, could look after things at the Bay during the winter months. There would be very little work for Joe to do. Perhaps he might be interested in some painting? Joe refused, saying he was afraid the Painters Union might object to someone performing their job for a lower salary. Ultimately, any further discussion on Joe's employment was tabled until September—a safe decision, as no one wished to antagonize the man whose services they relied upon during the summer months.[1]

Joe's reluctance to take on work beyond his job description was understandable. The early 1900s were boom years for construction in Vancouver, and a proliferation of low-paying jobs were being offered to Asian workers. Anti-Asian sentiment festered among the Caucasian populace. Conscious of the fact that he was in a racial minority, Joe may have felt some degree of concern on his own account. He had been subjected to the occasional derogatory remark, although there is no documented evidence to confirm that any previous episode was racially motivated.

Although both the Chinese and Joe at this time were sometimes seen as suspect "aliens," Joe himself had two curious runins with Chinese individuals, and it was clear that he wanted the upper hand. A report in the *Vancouver Daily Province* documents how Joe appeared in court on the morning of June 4, 1906, to testify that two "Chinamen," wandering around the bathhouse at ten o'clock one night, had resisted arrest. Sceptical of their explanation for being on the premises at such a late hour, Joe told them to "move along."

"I told them three times to move," he said, "but they said they had money and would do as they pleased. They thought they could bluff me, but let me tell you they can't bluff this chicken! I am a constable and I am going to see that things are all right around here!"

The defence counsel for the two men may have surprised Joe with his first question. "Don't you think they have a right to be around there?"

"They have a right if they behave themselves, but they have no right to run the town. They can't run this constable, anyway!" Joe's voice was firm and unfaltering, but the counsel pressed on with his questioning.

"You told them to move, did you?"

"Yes, I did, and they wouldn't move, so I took hold of them."

"Did you push them?"

"No, I didn't."

"Shove them?"

"No, but by right I ought to have shoved them."

By now the defence counsel could see that Joe was beginning to feel the pressure. "You gave them a small push, didn't you!" he said accusingly.

"Yes, a little push," Joe admitted. "They started home, then changed their minds. I told them I was a constable, and I arrested them, and delivered them to the station. It was my place to arrest them, and I did it!"

"Did you ever see this man before?" the counsel asked Joe, while pointing to one of the defendants.

"No. Don't know him at all."

"Did he know that you were an officer?"

"He ought to!" Joe retorted. "Everybody else in town knows me. I've been at the beach for over seven years."

At this point, the judge broke in and agreed that the men had been disrespectful of Joe's authority. He was glad that Joe had done his duty, but felt that the men had been punished sufficiently. The case was dismissed.

"Then you don't want my other witness?" said Joe.

"No," replied the judge. "He could not improve on what you have said."

Joe stepped out of the witness box, levelled a hard gaze at his two relieved adversaries, and left the court, perhaps feeling that justice had not quite been served.[2]

Joe's special-constable status was re-affirmed that fall, and the following year, on June 28, 1907, Joe found himself yet again in police court, relating how he had discovered a young Chinese man by the name of Mah Wing in the Park Board bathhouse dressing room at five o'clock in the morning.

"I asked him, what are you doing here? 'Going to have a swim,' the man replied. I told him, go long! You haven't had a bath in ten years! Where do you live? 'No sabez!' he says."

Mah Wing tried to make a run for it, but was quickly brought down by Joe and taken into custody. When searched at the station, he was found to have over a dozen keys in his possession. Joe was triumphant.

"There have been many towels stolen from the lockers of late, and I suspect the prisoner," Joe told the court. "This same man has a habit of hanging around the pavilion after the band concerts. And he is on hand early in the mornings. Go in to bathe? No, never!"

Mah Wing countered and explained that the keys found on him belonged to his lodging house on Pender Street. He admitted that he had gone to the bay rather early in the morning, but his objective was to seek work mowing lawns for local residents.

"I commend you for your vigilance, Mr. Fortes, but I fear you have no evidence," declared Magistrate Williams. "Case dismissed!"[3]

Once again, Joe saw his hopes of winning a conviction dashed by his inexperience with the demands of the legal system. If evidence was purely circumstantial or inconclusive, the case was often thrown out of court. As a special constable, Joe had not been submitted to the rigorous studies of trained city police officers, where he would have learned of such stipulations.

While Joe may have felt distrust for these particular Chinese individuals, it could not compare to the seething hatred that lurked among other Vancouver residents. On September 7, 1907, that hatred finally erupted into the open when what began as an orderly protest outside Vancouver City Hall swelled into an angry mob, and over fifteen thousand rioters stormed though the streets of Chinatown. Windows were smashed, counters were overturned and proprietors desperately seeking to protect their inventory were assaulted in their shop doorways, as hatred of non-white labour rose past the boiling point. Men with banners reading "Stand for a White Canada" tromped brazenly down the middle of Pender Street.

And where was Joe, with his gleaming brown skin, during all this chaos? It being a Saturday, he was in the water once again, as families were still coming to enjoy the last days of summer at English Bay beach.

CHAPTER 13

Triumph and Tragedy

On the afternoon of March 2, 1908, a boy by the name of Fred Owens came down to English Bay beach after school. There was a fierce squall blowing and spectacular waves were dashing against the shoreline. Far across the bay, about midway between Point Grey and Kitsilano, Fred could just barely make out a small sailboat through the afternoon haze. Something about the craft held his attention. It was beating heavily into the wind, with mainsail reefed. Moments later, Fred's eyes widened—the sailboat almost completely disappeared from view as it capsized.

Fred lost no time in finding Joe and reporting what he had seen. It being off-season, most of the rental rowboats were stored snugly inside the boathouse. Joe and one of the Simpson brothers raced to a lone boat lying on the beach. It only held one oar, but Joe did not want to waste precious minutes going off in search of another. The two men struck out across the bay in buffeting waves, taking turns to paddle furiously. It took almost half an hour to reach the overturned sailboat, where they found two very cold and exhausted Spanish fishermen clinging to the hull. A few more minutes and the men would likely have died of

Joe featured on a postcard with his friends on the beach. English Bay Pier is in background, c. 1908. (COURTESY BILL RAWNSLEY)

hypothermia. Joe's dramatic rescue made front-page news, and Vancouverites were in awe.[1] Perhaps there were other heroic lifeguards at other beaches, keeping watch, but none could compare to Joe Fortes.

The summer of 1908 saw larger crowds than ever flock to English Bay, and more improvements were being added to the beach. A one-hundred-yard-long pier jutting out into the water from Beach Avenue, about midway between Chilco and Gilford streets, was nearing completion at a cost of $52,768. The pier was a welcome addition for beachgoers, many of whom hailed from the United Kingdom, where such amenities were commonplace. It also meant an increased potential for trouble. Joe's unobstructed view of the water was now radically altered. Children could escape from inattentive parents and fall over the side. Devil-may-care teenagers could balance on the side rails and lose their footing. Joe had enough concerns to contact the City Police and Fire Committee. A brief item appeared among their April 2, 1908, communications:

> From Joe Fortes, applying for a boat for life saving purposes at English Bay. Referred to the Parks Commissioners with favourable recommendation from the Committee.[2]

On the morning of July 13, an unusually low tide revealed vast expanses of sandbar, the likes of which were seldom seen at English Bay. Mrs. George Richards walked slowly along the beach, her eyes carefully roving from right to left. She had lost an anchor from her sloop the previous day, and was hoping that it had washed ashore. She made inquiries with Joe, who told her that the anchor had indeed been found and he would take her up to the bathhouse where it was stored.

Out at the end of the new pier, the water was barely knee-deep. Swimmers and waders alike took advantage of the inviting scene, many venturing farther from shore than they had ever dared before. Two young women, sixteen-year-old Florine Anderson and eighteen-year-old Jean Sheppard, were among them, giggling like children as they ploughed through the shallows. A resident of Calgary, Jean and her husband had recently eloped and were enjoying their honeymoon in Vancouver. Mr. Sheppard had remained downtown this particular morning, while his young wife and her friend gave in to the irresistible appeal of the beach.

Some distance offshore from English Bay beach, there was a well-defined channel that led into False Creek. Dredging operations carried out the previous year had deepened the waterway to facilitate the ever-increasing size and number of vessels passing through. Locals were well aware of its presence, and only rarely did even the most capable swimmer venture out that far.

Near eleven o'clock cries went up. A young girl of seven was over her depth, along with Jean and Florine. The trio had stumbled into the trench and were screaming and thrashing about wildly. A nearby man concentrated his energies on the little girl, struggling furiously to keep her afloat. Three teenage boys, James Modershaw, Kenneth Phillips and Edward Aubrey, made a desperate attempt to rescue the other two, but by now Jean and Florine were fully panic-stricken.

"Lie on your backs and kick!" the boys yelled, trying to haul them in. The girls fought and thrashed so wildly that their would-be rescuers quickly grew exhausted. In danger of being dragged under themselves, the boys were forced to abandon their efforts. Up on the beach, some children ran to get Joe, who threw himself into the water and struck out for where the girls were last seen. For over an hour he dove and searched, but no trace could be found of the victims.[3]

Detective MacLeod of the city police force and Officer Munro of the RCMP were called to the scene. The Royal Vancouver Yacht Club contributed grappling equipment, and the dismal task of dragging for the girls' bodies commenced. Jean's distraught husband identified his wife's belongings from one of the bathhouse change rooms. It was well into the following day before Florine's body was discovered, not far from where she had initially gone under. Searchers speculated that Jean's body may have become lodged among rocks, and decided to try and dislodge it with charges of dynamite. It took three consecutive blasts and several more hours of dragging before the young bride's remains were located.[4]

It is said that when Joe's best efforts failed, his grief was "shattering to behold." When a reporter from the *Vancouver Daily News-Advertiser* approached him for comment on the day of the drownings, he vented his feelings in no uncertain terms.

"There was a time, when women and children were safe here because I had absolute authority and could compel them to keep within the limits of safety!" he said solemnly. "Now everything is changed. I have had my authority taken away and everybody knows that I am nobody. They won't listen to my advice, but if I had the proper power, I would compel them to do what they ought to do."

"Could you have saved them if you had had a boat, Joe?" the reporter asked.

"No man can answer that, but I'd have had a better chance!"[5]

Feeling a profound sense of obligation to protect each and every individual who patronized English Bay beach, Joe felt responsible for the deaths. The swimming members of the Vancouver Athletic Club were well aware of this, and secretly devised a plan in the hopes of easing Joe's guilt over his rare failure. On the evening of July 21, several club members converged on Joe's cottage just as he was settling in to dinner, and presented him with a handsome gold medal. Captain Stanley Warn spoke eloquently on the group's behalf of Joe's long years of service, and how much he was appreciated by his fellow swimmers. The medal, financed entirely by members of the Vancouver Athletic

Club, bore the club's crest on one side and an inscription on the reverse:

"Presented by the Vancouver Athletic Swimming Club to Joe Fortes for gallantry in saving life. July 1908."[6] Before long, news of Joe's award spread along the crowded promenade, and a large throng gathered outside the cottage, enthusiastically responding to the club members' calls for cheers. Utterly surprised and deeply touched, Joe displayed his characteristic dry wit, reminding the expert young swimmers before him that "he would be happy to give them his services at any time they should require it." Then,

In-the-water-pictures were becoming increasingly popular at English Bay. Joe with Rose Izen and an unidentified girl.
(COURTESY MICHAEL LEVENSTON)

as the cheers and applause rose to a crescendo, Joe's eyes welled, and his voice cracked with emotion as he thanked the crowd.

"I've always tried to do my best at the bay, and shall try to keep that reputation."[7]

The timing of Joe's award could not have been more appropriate, for repercussions of the tragedy continued to haunt him. The evening after the medal presentation, a report appeared in the paper, describing how "city authorities had refused to aid in the diving for and recovery of the bodies," and saying that "the costs of such a difficult and dangerous job must be paid for by the parties interested."[8] These were strong, critical statements— and as they were attributed to Joe, his presence was requested at a meeting of the City Police and Fire Committee on July 23 for a full explanation.

Joe stood firm before the committee and told his story. No, he had never made any statement to the effect that the City had refused all assistance that was possible to render. The statements quoted and attributed to him had never been made. Sergeant McRae of the City police force had been given instructions by Acting Mayor Stewart to spare no expense in recovering the bodies. Discussion turned to the reason for the drownings. Had Joe indeed alerted authorities to the existence of a deep hole in the bay and recommended that it be marked with a warning buoy? Joe again said that he had never made such a statement. He said that "there was no doubt in his mind that the women were seized in an undertow."[9] A brisk southeasterly wind, combined with the current coming out of False Creek, had resulted in a strong pull along the channel. During the numerous times that he dove down in search of the bodies he "had never felt anything so furious."

At this point in the meeting, Joe brought up his long-festering complaint. "If I still had the same powers of beach management that I had in years past, I might have been able to do more!" he declared. "Many accidents, even those of a simple nature, might have been prevented if the Parks Commissioners had not 'side-tracked' me from my former position!"[10]

It is difficult to know what exactly Joe meant by side-tracked. Perhaps he was intimating that his job description had been altered so many times in recent years that his ability to safeguard the beach was being severely compromised. A case in point was the recent tragedy. While he attended to "lost and found" duties, two girls were drowning. There was still the ongoing confusion with regard to Joe's accountability. Was he to take his orders from the Park Board or the city police? As a special constable what exactly were his restrictions? Some of his previous arrests had virtually been laughed out of court. Was he a valued member of the force, or were his policing services needed at all?

Sergeant McRae, in attendance at the meeting, tactfully suggested that in certain cases, it might be wiser for Joe simply to record names, information and to issue summonses as opposed to making on-the-spot arrests. Ultimately, it was the chief of police himself that settled the matter. All special constables were under his immediate control. Joe was to take his orders from the chief and no one else. All special constables had the authority to make arrests, and Joe was no exception. Joe confirmed that he was happy with this arrangement. Alderman Morton then spoke up in defence of Joe's ability to safely manage the beach. He argued that since the Park Board was in charge of English Bay, they should have a better-equipped lifeguard.

"Oh yes," Joe interjected. "Yesterday, I was provided with a boat."[11]

CHAPTER 14

"Merry Christmas, Joe!"

The popularity of English Bay led to increasing population density in the surrounding neighbourhood. Robson and Davie streets hummed with the steady circuit of streetcars. Saturday night revellers flocked to "The Prom," a dance hall perched at the end of the English Bay Pier. The Imperial Roller Skating Rink, sandwiched between Beach and Morton avenues, saw an ever-increasing crowd. Finding the peaceful environs of the emerging Shaughnessy neighbourhood more suitable to their tastes, many of the West End's fashionable elite began to vacate their stately Robson Street mansions. Rather than being placed in a non-lucrative, single-family occupancy market, the grand old residences were converted to apartments.

Joe demonstrates his diving skills for the admiring crowd.
(CVA 371-617)

Despite a lightening of attitudes towards mixed gender bathing and bathing attire, the desire for privacy while changing still reigned. In February of 1909, architect Edward Blackmore, fresh from his design of the Pantages Vaudeville Theatre on Hastings Street, was commissioned to draw up plans for a new bathhouse at English Bay. While the original Park Board bathhouse had been constructed in the popular "rustic lodge" style, Blackmore's facility would feature ornate Edwardian columns and balustrades akin to those of England's most popular seaside resorts. A *Vancouver Daily Province* article published on February 13, beneath a page-wide artist's conception of the new structure, gave a tantalizing description of its forthcoming amenities:

> Bathing Pavilion An Attraction—The building will be 276 feet long and the roof will be used as a promenade like the deck of a steamer. Perhaps there will be no greater attraction in Vancouver during the years to come than the new bathing pavilion which is to be erected on Beach Avenue facing English Bay, under the direction of Mr. E.E. Blackmore, the architect. It will be of concrete, painted white, and will be seen from a considerable distance of the boats entering the harbour. It will be necessary to excavate the bluff considerably. The back or north wall of the pavilion will be brought close to the sidewalk and probably not more than two steps above that level. Thus the concrete roof will become a fine promenade and furnished with seats. It will form an excellent point from which to view the beach and bathers.

> An office will be located in the middle, and the men's and women's dressing rooms are to the right and left. Each wing will contain 54 dressing rooms. There will also be shower baths. All of the dressing rooms will be well lighted and ventilated. Partitions separating the dressing rooms are to be built of "adamant" cement and a few inches above the floor and below the ceiling to permit passage of air. Doors, gratings and seats are so arranged as to allow the rooms to be easily and thoroughly cleaned.

Joe's house is discernible at the extreme south end of this unusual aerial view of English Bay beach featuring the 1905 and 1909 bathhouses, c. 1909. (CVA, Be P131)

"Kick yo' feet, chile!" (CVA 7-167)

The beach is to be approached by flights of steps from each side, and a broad terrace will run the full length of the building, 276 feet.[1]

The Simpson brothers continued to expand their boat rental services, and the Vancouver Amateur Swimming Club organized, among other popular spectacles, a marathon swim across English Bay to Kitsilano Beach. It is possible that Joe may have inspired this event with his frequent reflections on his infamous River Mersey crossing. In fact, Kitsilano Beach was coming into its own as a destination for recreational pursuits. A boathouse and dance hall had been in existence since 1905, and with streetcar service now available from downtown, the beach was becoming a popular alternative to busy English Bay.

In the fall of 1910, Mayor Louis Denison Taylor and his council decided that the time was long overdue for Joe to receive formal recognition on behalf of the City for his long years of service. Ex-mayor Fred Buscombe and Mr. Bernard McEvoy were appointed chairman and secretary of proceedings. At four in the afternoon of December 22, an audience packed the elegant chambers of the Board of Trade to witness the event. Buscombe addressed the gathering, acknowledging that he was "greatly pleased to fulfill the wishes of the people in presenting Mr. Fortes this afternoon." He went on to give a short but accurate account of the long years of service Joe had provided. "If in case some day Joe should choose to leave us, it would be a very hard matter to find a worthy substitute. His name has become a household word in nearly every family in this city."

Joe was invited to step up to the platform. He spoke emotionally of his gratitude for the honour, affirming that his years of services were "not to make myself a big man, but only for the benefit of the little ones, to whom my heart is attached and always will be." Joe went on to speak of his parents and his homeland. He spoke of his arrival in Vancouver, his early attempts to swim in the waters off Hastings Mill, and his delight in the discovery of English Bay beach. "I am sure that someday, when I go from where I never shall return, my mark will be clean and clear. God save the King!"[2]

Joe's gold watch, inscribed "Presented to Joseph Fortes by his many friends in Vancouver, B.C., Dec. 22, 1910." (COURTESY BUD KANKE)

Joe finished his speech and bowed graciously to hearty applause. Together with other dignitaries, Mr. Buscombe then presented Joe with a gold watch on a chain, a bank draft for $472 and a framed certificate. The certificate, delicately wrought by artist J. Kyle—with stylized calligraphy and whimsical watercolour paintings and ink sketches of Joe's little cottage, the Eng-

Joe's City of Vancouver certificate of appreciation, 1910.
(COURTESY NATIVE DAUGHTERS OF B.C. POST #1,
OLD HASTINGS MILL STORE MUSEUM)

lish Bay pier, nautical rope, seaweed, seashells and water nymphs flanking a life preserver—proclaimed the following words:

> Mr. Joseph Fortes, swimming instructor and life saver. This writing, with the gold watch, chain and bank draft for $472, which accompany it, is intended to express the high appreciation in which your services are held by the citizens and children of Vancouver, B.C. You have risked your life to save those of others, and in the heroic prosecution of your duties at English Bay, you have prevented many drowning accidents. As a teacher of swimming, you have rendered invaluable aid to learners, while your politeness and good nature have endeared you to all with whom you have come in contact. Childhood has been safe in your hands, you have the good opinion of all but the evildoer. We trust that you may long be permitted to exercise the duties which in the past you have so admirably performed.[3]

Donations towards the bank draft had been secretly collected over the past several weeks—a giant Christmas tip for the deserving Joe. Friends from near and far made their contributions. A telegram arrived from businessman Charles Gardner Johnston of California, who wired ten dollars, with an especially poignant message: "If this were my last $10, Joe would have half of it."[4]

Joe's picture, along with the full story of his special day, appeared in the December 23 edition of the *Vancouver Daily News-Advertiser*. Immaculately dressed in suit and tie, with new watch chain dangling from his waistcoat, he beamed proudly for the camera. Cash windfall aside, it appears that Joe's greatest reward came from the public adulation, in which he basked. Perhaps he at last felt vindicated for the affirmation and praise that sometimes had eluded him in his Trinidadian childhood.

CHAPTER 15

Life Goes On

Joe's pleasure over his formal recognition by the City was soon to be followed by heartbreak, with the death of his beloved friend Martha Scurry on February 12, 1911, at the age of sixty-one. Martha died from myocarditis, a congestive heart condition exacerbated by the asthma she had suffered from for many years. For Joe, losing Martha was akin to losing his own mother. Although she was not of the Catholic faith (the Scurry family were confirmed Baptists), Martha and Joe had shared a mutual love of serving God and community. It was Martha who had opened her home and heart to Joe, serving up generous helpings of hot food on frigid winter evenings, listening compassionately to his secret distresses and offering advice when wanted. She was a

Wedding photo of Cassie and Samuel Howard, c. 1908.
(COURTESY HOWARD FAMILY)

motherly presence when the young man may have felt a pang for the tropical breezes of his homeland. The Scurry children had grown and were raising families of their own. Cassie had married Samuel Howard and was now a busy mother to Melba and Charlie. Cassie and her family would continue to be a much loved and appreciated part of Joe's life.[1]

Meanwhile, English Bay and the West End continued to evolve. A series of beachside open-air concerts featuring Mr. F. Stuart-Whyte's The Versatiles and Tilley's Follies drew enthusiastic crowds. On December 20, 1911, Joe likely would have been among the throngs present at the official opening of Denman Arena, at the corner of Denman and Georgia. Billed as the largest indoor ice rink in the world, the Denman Arena provided seating for 10,500 fans to cheer on the Vancouver Millionaires hockey team. Henry Almond's Ice Cream did thriving business on Beach Avenue. The eight-storey Sylvia Court Apartments and six-storey Anglesea Lodge sprouted along Beach Avenue in 1912 as demand grew for residences with beachfront views. Twelve-year-old Sylvia Goldstein, daughter of Vancouver developer Abraham Goldstein and the namesake for his new apartment building would become a legendary swimmer in her own right under Joe's tutelage. The Sylvia Hotel flag flew at half-mast in April 2002 when Sylvia Goldstein Ablowitz died at the age of 102.

As 1911 drew to a close, the Vancouver Park Board released its first ever "Annual Report"—a glossy, multi-page document featuring photographs of well-known vistas around the city and an up-to-date status report on upkeep and recommendations for Vancouver's parks and recreational areas. With regard to English Bay and similar environs, the report's findings were unmistakable: "The cost of the upkeep of the beaches continues to

grow in proportion to their popularity. The need of more atten-
dants is urgent and to keep the bathing beaches in the condition
befitting their surroundings and importance, it will be necessary
in future to provide a much larger sum for their maintenance
than has hitherto been allowed."[2]

A lengthy list of the board's bylaws affirmed that, among
other things, certain expectations with regard to beachwear were
still in place:

> No person shall bathe or swim in the waters in, or adjoining any
> public park or place in the custody, care and management of the
> Board, unless clothed in the following manner hereinafter pre-
> scribed: Every person of the age of 15 or over, shall be clothed in
> a 2-piece bathing suit covering the body from the shoulders to
> the knees; Every person under the age of 15 in a 2-piece or single
> piece bathing suit covering the body from the shoulder to the
> knees.[3]

As the city continued to expand, the danger to constables such
as Joe also increased. Shock waves reverberated throughout the
Vancouver policing community and city as a whole when, on
March 25, 1912, Constable Lewis Byers became the first Vancouver police officer to be killed in the line of duty. Constable
Byers had been called to deal with a drunk and belligerent cus-
tomer who had run away after drawing a .38 revolver on staff
in a Powell Street liquor store. While attempting to apprehend
the man outside a nearby waterfront shack where he had taken
refuge, Byers was shot in the chest and neck at point-blank range
and died instantly. Other officers arriving on the scene were met
with more gunfire. They scrambled for cover and released a hail
of bullets. Holed up in his shack, the assailant perished.

A massive crowd paid final respects to Constable Byers on
April 1. At twenty years of age, he had barely completed five

months with the force. There is little doubt that Byers' murder would have had a psychological impact on Joe and his police colleagues. A *Vancouver Daily World* article recorded the scene:

> It was evident on all sides that the crowd manifested a genuine sorrow, intermingled with admiration of the heroic constable who had fallen martyr to the bullet of an assassin in the performance of his duty. But during the passing of that great pageant the hearts of the crowd were deeply touched with sincerest sympathy at the spectacle of the lonely figure of the young wife who passed by, weeping bitterly in a carriage, behind the hearse. Those few in the crowd who were able to obtain admittance into the church could not fail to notice, seated in the front pew in front of the casket containing the body of her husband, the sad drooping figure of Mrs. Byers who had been deprived of the gallant husband who had laid down his life in the execution of what is at all times a perilous duty.[4]

As special constable, Joe was authorized to carry a revolver, and no doubt felt a certain degree of vulnerability during his late night and early morning patrols. Fortunately, as English Bay was viewed as more of a family-oriented entertainment district, it did not often fall prey to the seamier side of Vancouver's existence.

Joe made a habit of reading the daily newspapers to keep abreast of local and world news. Like others, he would have been shocked and dismayed to learn that the massive ocean liner *Titanic* had struck an iceberg and sank in the early morning hours of April 15, 1912. In the days that followed, Joe was to learn that his old friend Hugo Ross was among those passengers unaccounted for and presumed drowned. Hugo had been holidaying with friends in Egypt and the Aegean region, but had decided to cut short his vacation due to illness. "We are on the

Boating at English Bay, post-*Titanic* disaster, with not a
lifejacket to be seen, 1912. (CVA 371-614)

last lap of the old lands and ready for Winnipeg and business!"
he had written on a postcard to some friends back home.[5]

The Simpson brothers' lease renewal of June 18, 1912, included a tally of eighty-five rowboats and canoes for hire at a
charge of fifty cents for three hours or one dollar per day.[6] Despite the *Titanic* tragedy, it appears that the importance of wearing a personal floatation device was yet to dawn on English Bay
boaters. A series of close-up, on-the-water photographs taken by
professional photographers from William John Cairns Ltd. at the
1912 summer swimming races offered proof. Gentlemen looked
handsome in their pressed suits and ties, ladies fashionably elegant in their puffy blouses and broad-brimmed hats, but not a
single life jacket could be seen amidst the occupants of a flotilla
of rowboats and canoes. Bathing costumes and towels were read-

ily available for rent at the bathhouses, but life jackets were scarce and still viewed as cumbersome, unattractive and unnecessary.

Perhaps a mite concerned over his ever-increasing responsibilities, Joe taught water-rescue techniques to his young pupils. One of the more popular events at the summer races was a lifesaving competition to see which "lifeguard" could tow his "casualty" back to shore the fastest. For all the dramatic developments of recent months—losing his dear friends Martha Scurry and Hugo Ross, as well as police force colleague Constable Byers—it appears that life went on relatively happily for Joe.

One January 1913 morning, a well-dressed gentleman came calling at Joe's cottage. He introduced himself as Noel Robinson, a historian and columnist whose work regularly appeared in several Vancouver newspapers. Noel explained that he would very much like to interview Joe for a weekly series he contributed to the *Vancouver Daily News-Advertiser*, called "The Story of My Life." Caught off-guard in the middle of his morning chores, Joe frowned. He was "not keen" on being interviewed. For the past several weeks, he had been attempting to compile a memoir of his own, and was not particularly eager to have some well-established writer show up unannounced and attempt to steal his thunder. Nonetheless, Noel Robinson's charm and affable manner eventually persuaded Joe to lower his defences and invite the writer inside.

The lengthy conversation that followed between the two men netted some results, even if they were not everything that Noel had hoped to uncover. While freely sharing details of his seafaring and Liverpool days, Joe had been careful not to let his reminiscences run away with him. As Robinson described, "Every now and again, Joe would break off in the middle of an attractive narrative with a deprecatory smile upon that kindly round face and remark, patting the top of the chest upon which he was sitting—within which the treasure evidently lay—affectionately, the while, 'Oh, but my lil' book—I means that one for my lil' book.'"

Reading between the lines of Robinson's article, it is possible to draw up a good impression of the middle-aged Joe. He was a kind-hearted man, perpetually beaming and polite, except when duty compelled him to adopt the stern demeanour of a police constable. He was well-organized and industrious, the cottage being spotlessly clean and tidy throughout, the small garden well-cared-for and much loved. Passionately nostalgic, he recalled for Robinson every minor detail of his first encounter with English Bay long years ago. "I landed just up here, this little bit of beach where my house now is, being the only bit of beach on English Bay then, and all was forest, with hardly a trail from English Bay to the town, and few explored that way." The framed certificate from the City of Vancouver occupied a prominent position on Joe's living room wall. He had also carefully preserved all the telegrams he had received during the 1910 public donation campaign.

Most telling were Joe's admissions that, after being in the water four to five hours a day, he was starting to feel a little sleepy. He now needed glasses to read with, and he was unimpressed by the newfangled strokes emerging on the swimming scene. "They last a little while and then they die away!" he remarked dismissively.

Unfortunately, much of Joe's private life remained a mystery. Did he ever take a holiday? Where were his off-duty haunts? Did he have any romantic liaisons? A man with the build of a

Joe's small garden was "well cared for and much loved."
c. 1915. (CVA, BU P111)

sumo wrestler must have had a hearty appetite. Did he cook for himself or have a favourite restaurant? We know that he regularly fished in the bay, often inviting two or three children to accompany him on the condition that they "sat still and behaved." His eyes would light up when presented with the gift of an orange or a box of chocolates from regular beachgoers. On at least one occasion he purchased a coconut, broke it open on a beach boulder and invited his friends to sample the tropical treat. It was said that he drank "his medicine," a cup of seawater, every day—a practice likely to be soon abandoned with the completion of an English Bay sewer outfall.

"The Story of My Life: Joe Fortes," as recorded by Noel Robinson, appeared in the January 19, 1913, Sunday Gazette edition of the *Vancouver Daily News-Advertiser*. Rich and colourful, packed with fascinating descriptions of St. George's Baths, *Robert Kerr* and Hastings Mill, the article closed with a lament: "This chat might be extended, full of anecdotes and interesting reminiscences for some columns more, but—botheration!—there is that Joe Fortes book looming in the background and the fear of stealing its thunder."[7]

Perhaps Joe decided that writing his autobiography was too onerous a task. Perhaps he laid it away in the deepest recesses of his chest, to work on "another day." The sad reality is that it has never been found.

CHAPTER 16

Home Fires

In the early hours of June 28, 1914, while waves lapped gently at the shore of English Bay and Joe slept soundly in his cottage, cracks of gunfire pierced the morning air in Sarajevo, Austria-Hungary. In the days and weeks that followed, the assassination of Archduke Franz Ferdinand and his wife Sophie, Duchess of Hohenberg, would trigger a worldwide chain reaction that no one would have imagined possible. On August 4, the United Kingdom formally declared war on Germany. Less than two weeks later, two 4.7-inch calibre naval guns were hoisted into position near Stanley Park's Siwash Rock, and given their first test firing. Resounding blasts echoed over the length and breadth of the bay.

Now into middle age, Joe was too old for active service. His emotions would surely have been in conflict as the first troop carrier pulled out of Vancouver on August 21. Hundreds of young, able-bodied men, including many of his former pupils, were headed overseas to the battlefront. The waning days of summer, which might have included pleasant family sojourns to English Bay, were being sacrificed in the name of duty to the "homeland." A hellish scene of gunfire, mud-laden trenches and mustard gas awaited.

As the 1915 season at English Bay approached, Joe made a request to City staff for a new lifeboat. On May 11, Public Utilities Committee members A.E. Lees and D.M. Stewart inspected the present boat and recommended that repairs be made by the Simpson brothers at a cost of eight dollars in lieu of a new boat.[1] It was wartime and frugality was paramount. Salaries for boat patrolmen at Second Beach and Kitsilano Beach were pegged at sixty-five dollars per month—a figure markedly down from Joe's 1900 salary of eighty dollars per month. The English Bay position was to be "left open for the present,"[2] indicating that Joe was in a category all his own. In another effort to reduce costs, the Public Utilities Committee granted J.R. Harter permission to offer private swimming instruction at English Bay at a charge of fifty cents per lesson.[3]

Wartime measures continued to affect Joe's well-ordered world. In mid-July, thirty-five men from the Canadian Army Medical Corp, 18th Field Ambulance, received City permission for use of one of the English Bay bathhouses between the hours of six and seven a.m., bathing suits included.[4] Soldiers were required to be in the peak of fitness before their deployment overseas. What better method of physical exercise was there than an early morning, uncrowded swim at English Bay beach in the height of summer?

J. Coughlan and Sons Shipyards was established on the south shore of False Creek, to build replacements for the increasing number of vessels damaged or sunk by German U-boats. Over the course of the war, Coughlan and Sons would become one of the largest ship-building companies in Canada. Joe would have a bird's-eye view of each newly completed Coughlan vessel being put through its wartime test runs in English Bay.

With so many fathers and sons overseas, those left behind struggled to maintain some sense of normalcy. Families continued to flock to English Bay, although emotions ebbed and flowed with the highs and lows of wartime. There was heady joy with the news of the Canadian capture of Vimy Ridge on May 15, 1916. Six weeks later, Dominion Day picnics were markedly subdued with word that the British military had suffered nearly 60,000 casualties, its greatest number in a single day, as the Battle of the Somme raged on the western front.

That same month, excitement was palpable throughout Vancouver. On the morning of July 19, Canada's governor general, the Duke of Connaught, his wife and fashionable twenty-five-year-old daughter, Princess Patricia, had arrived in Vancouver by train. The royal motorcade wound its way through the city, flanked by cheering throngs despite a heavy downpour. After various military receptions, stops at City Hall and the Cambie Street Grounds, the procession moved on to English Bay beach. The Duke of Connaught, third son of Queen Victoria, was Canada's first governor general of royal extraction. As Canada's Chief Scout—an honorary title inherited from his predecessor Earl Grey—he was also committed to working for the benefit of the Boy Scout movement nationwide. At precisely 4 p.m., under clearing skies, the royal party strolled the length of the pier between two lines of saluting Sea Scouts and were then treated to a dazzling display of diving and lifesaving skills.

Over the years, Joe had often fondly remarked to reporters about the times he had to jump in the water fully clothed to perform a rescue—occasionally in his Sunday best. Now, as the duke, duchess and princess watched in surprise, several lads jumped into the water fully clothed—a demonstration intended as an example of what lengths lifeguards had to go to when a life was at stake. Out on the water aboard his boat, Joe must have surely chuckled as his unorthodox training methods were played out before the royals. When the duke expressed concern about what Vancouver housewives would think of their son's drenched apparel, he was quickly reassured that these were "old clothes."[5]

On August 30, 1916, Joe's interview with a female reporter and her colleague, cartoonist James Fitzmaurice, was published in the *Vancouver Daily Province*, giving readers a whimsical glimpse of English Bay beach during wartime. Human interest stories had gained wide appeal at this time—a chance for readers to escape the harsh realities of front-page headlines and nightly lists of casualties. Full names of reporters were rarely published along with their stories. The author of this article was simply denoted by her initials, I.P. On the other hand, Fitzmaurice ("Fitz"), was a well-known *Province* cartoonist. He had been out of town for six years and was intrigued to see how the beach had evolved during his absence. The pair made their way to Joe's cottage for a pre-arranged meeting on his veranda. As they reasoned, "to write an article about English Bay without referring to Joe Fortes, would be like Hamlet without the Prince!"

Joe has a smile that makes his round face look like the sun shining through a smoke cloud; his figure is no longer willowy; his voice is hoarse and minatory as a distant foghorn. At all hours he may be seen in the water, floating at ease like a seal, or pulling about in the lifesaving skiff with one eye ever fixed on the outside fringe of bathers.[6]

The reporter asked Joe how life was treating him.

"Everything is lovely this season at the Bay. God has been good!" he told her cheerfully.

"Has anyone drowned?" she asked.

"No, there's been no drownings. Why there's been no drownings for six or seven years. We fish people out every day to be sure. The ladies now, they strike out to swim whether they can or not, and then when they can't find their feet, they lose their heads!"

Perhaps feeling that he had been somewhat discriminatory, Joe quickly added, "But I don't like those young fellows capsizing the raft! I'm disgusted to go among them. That is dangerous when there are so many people about. The raft is dangerous anyway—it's all waterlogged. The city ought to get a new one!"

"Do you like your work?"

"Yes ma'am, I like the work well enough, but it gets monotonous—very monotonous. These thousands of people every day, they get on the nerves and on many days I can't move along for the people. If I didn't come of a strong stock, I'd have wore out long ago. I'd be a wreck! Only the children keep me going. You might say children are my hobby. Now I'm teaching the children of the children I first taught here."

Joe went on to lament that the City didn't pay him enough to live on. It was very hard to get by, and it was especially hard to

"Yes ma'am, I get on all right with the children!"
(VPL SPECIAL COLLECTIONS, VPL 83598)

have anything for the children. He was often asked to finance an ice cream cone or a streetcar ride home. Joe had become a father figure to dozens of families torn apart by war. As if on cue, a little girl appeared at the edge of the veranda. The reporter made note of the lively conversation that ensued:

"Joe—oh Joe!"

About half a dozen children were gathered behind her.

"Are you going to swim today, Joe?" she asked.

Joe's smile broke out full.

"Oh, about three, probably!" he replied.

"All right, we'll meet you then!" Off she ran with her young friends in tow.

"Yes ma'am, I get on all right with the children!" Joe nodded to the reporter.

True to his word, Joe was soon down on the sands, attired as always in the woollen one-piece bathing suit that accentuated every ripple of his husky frame.

Fitzmaurice went on to produce several sketches to accompany his colleague's article. Among them was a self-portrait of a gentleman in a pinstriped suit, straw boater perched jauntily atop his head, admiring a bathing-suit-clad Joe standing attentively on the shore. "What perfect lines!" the caption read.

As dusk descended at English Bay beach, bonfires were lit to ward off the late summer evening chill. Young couples were visible the length of Beach Avenue, ladies in flapper dresses and young men in uniform, strolling beneath the gaslights or exchanging light-hearted small talk over desserts in the ice cream parlours. The reporter continued recording her observations:

> By the rules of romance they should have been saying good-bye with tears and sighs and protestations of faithfulness until death. There were soldiers everywhere, walking mostly two by two. One could pick out the newest by their looks of unconscious heroism, the old hands by nothing but their khaki. One, an officer too by his shoulder straps, took no shame to be seen while wheeling a baby carriage, the while he walked by his pregnant wife.[7]

Down on the beach, the bonfire flames danced higher.

CHAPTER 17

The Bracelet

Through the years that followed, one of Joe's greatest pleasures was to see Cassie Howard and her growing brood of children arrive at English Bay for one of their infrequent summer excursions. After the death of Martha Scurry, Joe had remained close to her daughter Cassie. Joe considered the Howards his family, "his people," as he put it. As the Howard family lived on Nanaimo Street in East Vancouver, a day's outing to the beach required two streetcar rides. Cassie planned the trip meticulously. The wicker picnic basket had to be packed with enough food for lunch and dinner—a massive potato salad, ham sandwiches, wild blackberry pie and enough lemonade to slake the thirst of a regiment. Often there would be a last-minute scramble when it was discovered that one of the children had outgrown their bathing suit and a makeshift one would have to be improvised from their father Samuel's cast-off underwear.

Upon their arrival at the beach, the Howards would immediately look for Joe. More often than not he would be out in his rowboat, the midday sun glistening off his balding head and muscular body as he kept a watchful eye on the hordes of children that frolicked all around him.

"Hi, Joe!"

Upon noticing the frantic waving at the water's edge, Joe would row in to greet Cassie and her family. There was little time for pleasantries while he was on duty, so arrangements were made to meet at his house at the end of the day. Young Goldvine Howard especially looked forward to the evening visits with Joe:

> I remember well how happy we were to be invited to Joe's home. Mother always insisted on us sitting on chairs and not wandering around touching things, as one of the boys of the family would probably have broken something. I sensed that we were in a real bachelor's haven—there were all sorts of unusual articles that had to be observed at a distance; a pipe and tobacco (something very foreign to our home), ship models, shells, and those intriguing glass paper weights, jars of candy and fancy tins of biscuits for tea. If we were patient enough, Joe would remember to pass around the biggest and best chocolates of one's life!

Even though a child, Goldvine could see that Joe struggled with demons from his past:

> Joe confided in Mother about his life and ambitions and any problems he had like chaperoning late night revellers on the beach, about being estranged from his family, about his brother who was studying medicine in England, about his own humble job. His family would think, "What's a lifeguard?" He was ob-

viously not the clever favourite son and had probably left home at an early age to go to sea, and seek his fortune beyond the shadow of his brother.[1]

Joe made a habit of early morning beach combings, generally to ensure that nothing hazardous had floated in with the evening tide or been left behind by careless beachgoers. During one of his evening visits with the Howards, he brought out a surprise. "Here is a bracelet I found on the beach," he told them. "I would like one of the children to have it." Everyone gathered around to admire the bracelet. It was fashioned from sterling silver with a classic design and three little dangling hearts of silver. The spacing of the hearts indicated that additional hearts had become detached and lost. Joe had made many inquiries in an effort to locate the bracelet's rightful owner, but to no avail.

The bracelet found on the beach by Joe.
(COURTESY HOWARD FAMILY)

Everyone unanimously agreed that Melba, eldest of the Howard daughters, would be the natural recipient of the bracelet. Goldvine watched in awe, and perhaps with a little bit of envy, as it was slipped onto her sister's wrist. The children tried to conjure up romantic notions of the bracelet's origin. Perhaps it had belonged to some lady of great importance—like a society matron, or perhaps even a duchess? Joe was visibly pleased to be able to give a gift of beauty and value to one of Cassie's children. In time, Melba would tire of wearing the bracelet and pass it along to a delighted Goldvine, who wore it continuously for the rest of her life.[2]

CHAPTER 18

Decline

By the time he reached his early fifties, Joe had spent nearly half his life teaching three generations of Vancouver children to swim. He was known throughout the city and beyond. Noted city photographer Philip Timms' photograph of Joe in midair off the English Bay diving platform had even been featured on a Vancouver postcard, bearing the caption, "Our Friend Joe."

For some time, there had been talk of constructing an indoor swimming venue at English Bay. Park Board staff quietly began to weigh the options. On March 25, 1918, a preliminary list of recommendations was drawn up, calling for "an indoor heated salt water swimming bath, thirty-five feet in width by one hun-

"Our Friend Joe" postcard, c. 1906. (CVA, AM 1052, P-38)

dred feet in length, a spectator gallery, Turkish bath, palm room, showers, toilets, dressing boxes and a concert hall."[1] The project apparently died on the vine and it would be another nine years before the privately developed Crystal Pool opened on Beach Avenue.

On May 14, 1919, Joe addressed City Council, asking for an increase in salary. It was moved by Alderman Kirk, seconded by Alderman McRae, "that the City Comptroller be instructed to place Joe Fortes on the payroll at an amount equal to other civic employees similarly situated."[2] The motion was carried. Unfortunately, no personnel records have survived to confirm if Joe did indeed receive a raise, in light of this decision.

The summer of 1919 was the busiest ever at the beach. Crowds were so thick that on some occasions it was nearly impossible to reach the water's edge. On July 19, a Great Peace Celebration saw buildings decorated with flowers and bunting up and down Beach Avenue. Fireworks lit up the evening sky over English

Bay. The Great War armistice had long passed, but a joyous, mid-summer celebration of a perceived new era of peace seemed fitting and therapeutic.

Joe was fascinated by the growth of Vancouver, and confidently predicted that someday the city would extend as far out as New Westminster. But with English Bay crowds increasing in size from one summer to the next, Joe began to feel his energies wane. During the off-seasons, it was becoming an increasingly onerous task to keep his Beach Avenue home stocked with enough firewood to ward off the winter cold. Late in the fall of 1919, he developed a severe cold, which grew worse after he came to the rescue of a Japanese fishing crew whose vessel had run aground in a gale off Second Beach. A reporter, interviewing Joe for the November 9 edition of the *Vancouver Sun*, detailed the story: "He went out and helped bring the shipwrecked fishermen to safety. This aggravated his cold so seriously that he was confined to his bed, suffering from complications, which threatened his life." But then the reporter, displaying the attitude prevalent among beachgoers, brushed off the incident, assuming that the legendary Joe was impervious to any permanent harm: "But now, Joe is around again, and he is ready for whatever may arise, whether it be to go out in a storm and bring aid to some mariner in distress or whether it be to keep the rising generation out of mischief along the beach."[3]

"Mischief" took on a whole new meaning on New Year's Day of 1920, when an exuberant Peter Pantages (nephew to the owner of the Pantages Theatre) and ten friends made a mad dash from the basement of the Sylvia Hotel, straight into the bone-chilling waters of English Bay. Whooping with laughter, they splashed about while onlookers stared in astonishment from the shore. No media was on hand to record the event, but the

Joe's cane.
(COURTESY JOE FORTES
BRANCH LIBRARY)

first annual "English Bay Polar Bear Swim" would grow to become a cultural phenomenon, attracting thousands of participants in future years.[4] While Joe enjoyed a close friendship with Peter, it is unlikely that he participated in this revelry.

The early stages of rheumatism were invading Joe's limbs. Some friends pooled their finances to purchase him a walking cane, complete with a silver band near the top bearing the engraving, "Joe."[5] By the fall of 1921, it was clear that he needed it. In a surprising move, Joe also took time off work to travel to Harrison Hot Springs—his first vacation that anyone could ever recall—indicating just how exhausted he really was. Long recognized for their healing properties, first by the Stó:lō Nation and Fraser Valley settlers, later by Vancouverites eager to treat a wide variety of maladies, the Harrison Hot Springs were readily accessible via gravel road from the CPR station at Agassiz. Economic disaster had struck the town of Harrison Hot Springs one year previously when fire, believed to have been caused by a defective flue, levelled the fashionable three-storey St. Alice Hotel. With no new accommodations in the works, it appears likely that Joe was a guest in one of the numerous summer cottages constructed over the years by wealthy Vancouver businessmen.

However much Joe enjoyed his vacation, the rheumatism continued. To worsen matters, early in January of 1922, he contracted mumps. Steadfastly refusing to leave his home, Joe took to his bed and kept his condition as secret as possible. A substitute special constable was brought in to fulfill his patrol obligations. On the evening of January 16, Joe deteriorated. An ambulance was sent for, but he stubbornly refused to be loaded aboard until he had given elaborate instructions to his replacement.

Vancouver General Hospital's Heather Pavilion was a grandiose 1906 structure located in the residential neighbourhood of Fairview. Nurse Beatrice Wood was on duty when Joe was brought in on a gurney. Hoping to ease his fears, she told him that he had taught her how to swim. "I won't teach no one no more, Missy!" he replied.[6]

A brief news article appeared in the January 17th edition of the *Vancouver Daily Province*:

> English Bay Joe is seriously ill in the General Hospital. To the three generations of Vancouver kiddies who learned swimming under his watchful care, to the tens of thousands who count themselves as friends of the veteran coloured lifeguard Joe Fortes, the news comes as a distinct shock. Already the General Hospital has been besieged with telephone calls as to his condition, and his bedside is heaped with flowers and other offerings from old and young of all classes and creeds.[7]

A similar report appeared in the *Vancouver Sun*, along with the ominous news that doctors feared Joe was fighting pneumonia.[8]

Not to be deterred from his work even when lying in a hospital bed, Joe requested that additional instructions for his replacement be telephoned to police headquarters. An update on his condition was issued the following day in the *Vancouver Daily Province*:

"Ah'm Alright" Says Joe Fortes, But Doctors Keep Him

Joe Fortes, the veteran coloured lifeguard of English Bay, who was taken ill last Monday, is in a much improved condition at the General Hospital today. "Ah'm alright now," Joe says, "but those doctors won't let me out for a while yet." Joe is fretting at his enforced absence from duty, and it will not be long before he is back in his little cottage at the Bay if he has any say in the matter.[9]

No further reports were issued on Joe's progress but on January 22, headlines blazed with the death of the well-loved humanitarian, Pope Benedict XV. The leader of the Catholic Church had succumbed to pneumonia. While there is little doubt that Joe would have received regular updates on the status of English Bay beach, this sad piece of world news may have been tactfully concealed from him.

CHAPTER 19

"The Passing of a Great Soul"

Late in January of 1922, Cassie Howard received a surprise telephone call from Vancouver General Hospital. Joe Fortes was ill and asking to see her. It appears that until now, Cassie had been unaware of Joe's condition. She was a busy housewife with toddler Barbara now added to the Howard clan. Cassie literally dropped everything she was doing and rushed to the hospital.

Joe had recovered somewhat over recent days but confided in Cassie that he was still afraid he was going to die. Cassie asked if there was any family member that she could write to, but he said no. It appears that all family contact had been broken. Joe beckoned her closer and explained that if anything happened to him, she was to have his old waistcoat. Joe had worn the coat constantly when not in his swimming attire, and for good reason. Into the lining, he had sewn his fortune.

"Cassie, you will never have to worry about money. I want you to have it."

Cassie humoured Joe, saying that she would remember his wishes to take the coat. Inwardly, she believed that he was regaining his strength and would soon be back at English Bay where he belonged. "If you need me, get one of the nurses to phone me and I'll come," she added.[1]

On Saturday, February 4, having prepared dinner in advance, Cassie decided that she would pop over to the hospital to see how Joe was getting along. Leaving the elder children in charge, she boarded the streetcar for the short journey from Nanaimo to Heather. Later, she would call her spontaneous visit a premonition. She arrived to find Joe delirious with pneumonia. An on-duty nurse told her that the end was near.

"Joe!" she called softly, sitting at his bedside. "It's Cassie."

Joe did not reply, but seemed to be aware that she was there.

"Would you like me to sing a hymn for you?"

Joe made an effort to speak but couldn't find the strength. Cassie began to sing one of her favourite hymns, "Lead Kindly Light Amid Encircling Gloom":

> Lead, kindly light, amid encircling gloom;
> Lead thou me on
> The night is dark and I am far from home;
> Lead thou me on.
> Keep thou my feet, I do not ask to see,
> The distant scene: One step enough for me.[2]

Joe passed away peacefully a few moments later on February 4, 1922, as Cassie continued singing.

Although cause of death was officially recorded as cerebral hemorrhage and arteriosclerosis, it could arguably be said that Joe's passing was largely due to the recent years of taxing his body well beyond its capabilities. On Sunday, February 5, Police Chief Anderson and Deputy Chief Leatherdale entered Joe's cottage, collected his badge and revolver, boarded up the windows and locked the doors. The following day, at a meeting of the City Council's Harbour, Industries and Employment Committee, it was recommended "that the City Council attend the funeral of the late Joe Fortes, lifeguard at City Bathing beaches, meeting at the Holy Rosary Church on Tuesday, February 7 at 10 a.m. and that the City Comptroller be authorized to forward a suitable wreath for the occasion."[3]

Civic funerals were a rarity in Vancouver, generally being reserved for high-ranking politicians or others of similar background. A notable exception was the funeral for poet Pauline Johnson, which had taken place on March 10, 1913. Another exception would be Joe's funeral. The City spared no expense in ensuring that Joe would be given a fitting tribute. Alderman Frank Woodside, whose six children had all been taught to swim by Joe, took charge of coordinating plans.

Funeral arrangements were published in the *Vancouver Sun*[4] and *Vancouver Daily Province*.[5] The Holy Rosary Cathedral pews were full well before the scheduled service, with people standing two and three deep in the aisles. At 9:30 a.m., the cathedral organist, Miss Adele Heritage, defied convention by playing a familiar plantation melody, "Old Black Joe." A *Vancouver Daily Province* reporter chronicled the moment:

> Beautifully and reverently the theme was worked into the fabric of the music, first quietly and in a subdued minor key, a key of sorrow and regret and farewell. Gradually, this note gave place

to a stronger tone and a suggestion of rest and work accomplished came from the deep heart of the organ, and finally, all minor and sorrowful modes of expression were discarded and I hear their gentle voices calling Old Black Joe in a glorious major burst of triumph through the church as the western doors opened wide and the casket containing all that was mortal of the old lifeguard was carried up the aisle.[6]

Joe's casket, piled high with flowers, was borne into the sanctuary by his closest friends from the Vancouver Police Department: Inspector H.W. Long, Sergeant John Deacon, and Police Constables J.G. McLellan, H. Morrison, A. Nickerson and R.P. McGrenara. Reverend Father Thayer conducted high mass, after which Reverend Father O'Boyle gave absolutions. The Holy Rosary Men's Choir sang selections of hymns. At the close of the ceremony, Father O'Boyle ascended the pulpit to address the crowd:

> You are assembled today to do honour to old Joe. In doing this, you are also honouring yourself, as coming here to observe the passing of a guardian of young Vancouver. He was a man who was truly built in the image of God. His one aim and joy in life was to serve. He was an example of industry, self-denial and charity: He gave his best to all and without distinction for the sake of the community. This great gathering is evidence, to me, of the fine spirit of brotherly love abiding in the great heart of Vancouver, when so many of all classes of our citizens leave their affairs to honour one who for so long gave his whole life to safeguarding the lives of others.[7]

The cortège through the downtown streets was lengthy and solemn. Some ten thousand onlookers bundled against late winter sleet lined the route along Dunsmuir to Granville, north to Hastings and east to Main. As marshall of the funeral procession, Senior Traffic Inspector Hood led the way on horseback, followed by the Elks Brass Band playing Chopin's funeral march. Joe's hearse, flanked by an honour guard of uniformed Vancouver police constables, travelled slowly behind. Through the efforts of Chairman W.C. Shelly, of the Vancouver Park Board, and his commissioners, several poignant personal touches were added. Joe's lifeboat followed the hearse bedecked with flowers and evergreen boughs from Stanley Park. Joe's off-hours had been few in the course of his career, but he had loved to stroll the park trails when time permitted. A set of oars, each interlaced with vines from Joe's beloved garden, lay across the seats, paddles pointed astern. Vancouver Mayor Tisdall, the city aldermen, members of the School Board, Park Board and Police Commission, as well as many of Joe's colleagues from the police force, representatives from the Vancouver Amateur Swimming Club and members of various fraternal organizations all made their way to Mountain View Cemetery, Joe's final place of rest.

Hundreds of school children had clamoured for permission to attend Joe's funeral, but city officials stopped short of declaring a full school closure. As many reasoned, "Joe would never have permitted children to go out in bad weather." However, between 10:40 and 10:45 a.m., teachers were asked to call upon their pupils for a moment of silence in tribute to Joe. Schools all over Vancouver complied.

Joe's grave marker was a simple and unobtrusive stone rectangle bearing the capital letters "JOE."[8] It was virtually hidden amidst a vast array of floral wreaths from Vancouver citizens and organizations: Mr. and Mrs. Bell-Irving, the Vancouver City Policemen's Union, Mr. and Mrs. Harry Abbott, the Knights of Columbus, the City of Vancouver, the Chief of Police and staff, the Board of Parks Commissioners, David and Edith Oppenheimer. There was also a wreath from "the Howard children."

Joe's 1922 and 2005 gravestones in Mountain View Cemetery, Vancouver, B.C. (MOUNTAIN VIEW CEMETERY, 1919-B-40-9)

In his final sermon at graveside, Father O'Boyle reiterated his funeral message: "You do honour not only to 'Old Joe,' who has just gone out with the tide on the great ocean of eternity, but to yourselves, indeed, in gathering to tender solemn homage of respect for the passing of a great soul."[9]

CHAPTER 20

Joe's Legacy

With no will or final instructions to refer to, officials were at a loss regarding the distribution of Joe's estate as there was no known heir. In a moving tribute published not long after the funeral, Noel Robinson made a brief mention of Joe's unwillingness "to engage in a lawsuit in the island of Trinidad, where as the eldest son, he and his sister feel that he was entitled to the estate left by his father and now in other hands."[1] It appears that Joe's ties with his Trinidadian roots were long severed. Probate documents filed "In the Matter of the Administration Act" and "In the Matter of the Estate of Joe Fortes, Deceased" confirmed that he had $141.91 cash on hand, $51.97 deposited in the Royal Bank, and personal effects valued at a total of $63.50.

By the time bills were paid off—$185.25 for burial, a $14.75 General Hospital fee and $24.29 owed to someone by the name of Shang Hattie for services unknown—Joe's net worth amounted to $33.09.[2] After a time, Cassie Howard made inquiries about the waistcoat with its hidden cash, but no one knew of its whereabouts.[3]

Representatives from the newly formed Native Daughters of British Columbia Post #1, a ladies' organization dedicated to the preservation of British Columbia history, obtained Joe's oil lamp, and his much-treasured framed certificate from the City of Vancouver. These artifacts would eventually find their way to the Old Hastings Mill Store Museum, formerly the Hastings Mill Store, where Joe had obtained his welcoming advice from storekeeper Calvert Simson so many years previously.

Everyone agreed that a suitable, lasting memorial for Joe would not only be in order, but of absolute necessity. Ideas were debated, and on January 15, 1925, an editorial appeared in the *Vancouver Sun*:

> Pioneers of Vancouver will raise a fund to erect a memorial to Joe Fortes, the old black man who for many years presided at English Bay. Such a memorial is in the interests of good citizenship. No city, province or nation can afford to be without its heroes. Hero worship is the most binding factor in any social organization.[4]

The Kiwanis Club of Vancouver was delegated to administer the fund. It was decided that a sum of five thousand dollars would be required to construct a public water fountain in Alexandra Park, mere steps from Joe's Beach Avenue cottage. By April of 1926, the fund had grown to $1,506, by early May, $2,457. Donations large and small came in: $250 from Vancouver City Council, $25 from Bowman Storage and Cartage Company and

$1.00 from E.M. Bryant. Beneath a column headlined "MORE FUNDS NEEDED," the *Vancouver Daily Province* recorded one of the more poignant contributions from a young lad. "Is this where you take subscriptions for the memorial for 'Old Joe Fortes'?" he asked. "Well, I want to give this fifty cents to the fund. It's not much, but Joe pulled me out of the water once and I want to do what I can."[5]

Italian sculptor Charles Marega was the natural choice to create a memorial for Joe. The Kiwanis Club had recently sponsored a contest, searching for the ideal artisan to create a memorial sculpture of President Warren Harding, first U.S. president to visit Canada. A judging panel of well-known sculptors from across North America selected Marega as the winner. Public acclaim for the Harding memorial was so great that Charles Marega and his wife decided to become Canadian citizens.

Originally, Marega's plan was to have a three-dimensional statue, featuring a bronze cherub perched atop a granite tableau,[6] but cost restraints or other factors may have forced him to adopt a simplified version. The final result featured a bronze relief portrait of Joe dressed in his familiar waistcoat and tie with a hint of a smile, and three cherubic children cavorting in the shallows beneath. The reverse side of the fountain bore the following inscription: "This fountain erected by the citizens and children co-operating with the Kiwanis Club of Vancouver commemorates the life and deeds of Joe Fortes for many years guardian of this beach. Little children loved him. A.D. 1927."

On the evening of Friday, June 24, 1927, the memorial fountain to Joe Fortes was unveiled before a large crowd in Alexandra Park. In their first public appearance, the newly formed First National Boys Band of the Native Sons of British Columbia played "Oh Canada," "The Maple Leaf Forever" and other select

Joe's memorial fountain in Alexandra Park.
(COURTESY DOUG SMITH)

pieces. Led by Mr. William Hennessy, the audience joined in a rousing chorus of "Old Black Joe." Past Kiwanis President Charlie Bruce made the unveiling speech: "Under a dusky skin beat the heart of unalloyed gold. Sweet tempered, ever patient, always smiling, Joe Fortes radiated happiness, and so garnered a harvest of love and confidence from the children around him. A native of Trinidad, West Indies, son of a Spanish mother and a West Indian farmer, Joe, at the age of 16, harkened to the call of the sea and in a windjammer sailed to Liverpool."

Charlie Bruce went on to talk about Joe's *Robert Kerr* days, his appointment as lifeguard and duties as a special constable.

"His vigilance and gallantry averted twenty-six certain drownings. I now dedicate this monument to perpetuate the memory of Joe Fortes, the children's friend and a man among men."

Vice-President of the Kiwanis Club R. Nicholson then officially presented the memorial to Alderman Henry Elston Almond, who accepted it on behalf of the City of Vancouver. On behalf of Vancouver's coloured population, many of whom were in attendance, the Reverend U.S. Robinson was invited to say a few words. He spoke of Joe's unselfish spirit, "which prompted you to give honor where honor is due. You have expressed to the world that you recognize the essentials of life are love, loyalty, devotion and honor, whether these be found in prince or peasant." Reverend Robinson pointedly reminded his rapt listeners to "follow their own aspirations, of the same noble purpose as Joe's."[7]

It will never be known exactly how many children Joe taught to swim, or how many of those children grew up and passed along his teachings to others. Joe's Beach Avenue cottage was demolished and burned where it stood sometime in 1928. A small grove of trees near a rock-laden promontory at the southerly end of English Bay beach now marks the spot. Among those rocks would likely be found fragments of the giant boundary rock that once stood between the men's and lady's swimming beaches. There is no trace to be found of Joe's autobiography. Likely written in Spanish, perhaps it was cast aside by someone unable or unwilling to recognize its historical value.

Artifacts traceable to Joe are few and far between: his framed certificate from the City of Vancouver, his oil lamp and a photograph continue to reside at the Old Hastings Mill Store Museum,

Joe's Morris chair, c. 1900-1920.
(MUSEUM OF VANCOUVER COLLECTION, H986.64. 1A-B)

under the watchful stewardship of Native Daughters of B.C. Post #1. The gold watch given to him at the 1910 city reception is still in excellent condition under private ownership. A Morris chair—remarkably well-preserved, save the rings burned onto one wooden arm where Joe rested his hot drinks—and a handkerchief which he gave as a prize at a Sunday school picnic reside at the Museum of Vancouver. Joe's cane can be found on display at Joe Fortes Branch Library. Intriguingly, a weather-beaten rowboat hangs suspended from the ceiling of Vancouver's Mill Marine Bistro. While there is no paper trail to verify its authenticity, the craft is reputed to have been one of the city's first commissioned lifeboats and therefore used by Joe. After being restored several times over the years, it was banished to the English Bay

The lifeboat possibly used by Joe.
(COURTESY MILL MARINE BISTRO)

bathhouse in the late 1990s. It became a permanent fixture of the Mill Marine Bistro when the Coal Harbour eatery opened in 2003. On the subject of boats, the *Robert Kerr*—which saw new life as a coal barge in the years following its 1885 condemnation, foundered and sank on an uncharted reef off Thetis Island on the night of March 4, 1911. Today the decaying wreck lies in 10 to 20 metres of water—a popular dive site identified by an Underwater Archaeological Society of B.C. historic plaque. The *Robert Kerr* ship's bell—preserved in the Vancouver Maritime Museum, continues to be ceremoniously rung every April, at the Vancouver Historical Society's annual Incorporation Day Luncheon.

Historical retrospectives on Joe continue to appear in local newspapers periodically. A West End library and a restaurant are named in his honour. In 1986, the Vancouver Historical Society formally declared Joe "Vancouver Citizen of the Century."[8] In September of 2005, Tom Crean, owner of Kearney Funeral Services, provided financing for a new grave marker for Joe at

Mountain View Cemetery. The new marker, carved in blue granite reminiscent of the ocean, features Joe's full name, Seraphim "Joe" Fortes, etched between images of a lifeguard's chair and crucifix.[9]

Perhaps Joe's most fitting tribute is the lengthy list of memories recorded first-hand by those individuals fortunate enough to have shared time with him. Goldvine Howard and her younger sister Barbara—of Joe's Vancouver "family"—have done much to keep Joe's memory alive over the years. Ian Nicholson recalled watching Joe rescue two men from an overturned boat: "He swam back to shore with the weakest of the pair clinging to his shoulders while monitoring the other, and then insisted they both come into his cottage to get warm and dry."[10] Mary Elizabeth Colman was one of many fortunate children invited to sit in Joe's rowboat when he went out fishing in the evening. "Though he was so kindly, Joe was not indulgent. In the rowboat you sat still," she recalled.[11] Mike Crammond told of bringing Joe an orange, and how gratefully the lifeguard accepted it.[12]

A short letter by Frank Farley appeared in a March 1964 issue of the *Vancouver Province*: "In the summer of 1909 I started to swim out to the diving float at English Bay, which was held by a cable. At the time, I was not a strong swimmer, and before reaching the float, I wanted to rest. I took hold of the cable, but it proved to be quite slack, and I went under. Old Black Joe got me out."[13]

Retired *Vancouver Sun* reporter Pat Slattery told how, at the age of six, he learned to swim from atop Joe's big shoulders: "He used to tell me to climb on, and he would swim into deep water and toss me off. I'd dog paddle back to him, always feeling safe. Saturday, I would sweep out his cottage, proud to be doing him a turn."[14]

Barbara Howard with a photo of her sister Goldvine, both members of
Joe's Vancouver "family," January 17, 2011. (HOWARD FAMILY)

George Burrows, who retired in 1971 as supervisor of Vancouver's beaches and pools, recalled rowing over to English Bay
beach with extra towels from the Kitsilano bathhouse: "Joe, I
got towels, I'd say, and he'd turn to the people in the water calling, 'Make way for this boat! Make way for this boat!'"[15]

Pat Prowd was only a three-year-old toddler when, while her
mother enjoyed tea with friends on the English Bay pier, she
wandered away and fell into the deep water. Moments later, she
felt a huge hand under her and as it scooped her out of the water,
she heard Joe's booming voice yell, "Kick baby, kick!"[16]

Betty McLean was only five years old when she met Joe. A
few nights before Christmas of 1921, she joined four or five other
excited kids who waited and watched as Joe lit gas lamps along

Beach Avenue. When he was finished, he would give them each a nickel to spend on Christmas candy. When Joe died later that winter, Betty's parents told their saddened daughter of the song "Old Black Joe," and its comforting refrain. For years afterwards, Betty believed the words were written especially for her lamplighter friend.[17]

Impresario Hugh Pickett, who socialized with the likes of Marlene Dietrich, Ginger Rogers and Katharine Hepburn, was another of Joe's swimming pupils. He recalled how as a child he could knock on Joe's door, unexpected, and how thrilled he was to be invited to enter the cottage and be treated to some candy or a Coke. It was Mr. Pickett who asserted that Joe's surname "Fortes" was typically pronounced "Fortz," although many variations have emerged over the years.[18]

Renee Jensen's recollections were particularly heartfelt: "In 1920, when I was just six, my two brothers and I met Joe. My oldest brother was a polio victim. Joe's patience and kindness endeared him to me for all time. My brother could now float and learned to swim safely."[19]

One imagines that somewhere, amidst the noise and commotion, the traffic and high-rises, the summer fireworks, New Year's Day Polar Bears, popcorn stands and rollerbladers of twenty-first-century English Bay, a rotund gentleman with chestnut brown skin and a gleaming bald head still patrols his beat. Perhaps above all the din, if you stop and listen hard, you might still hear a streetcar bell clang, the rhythmic stroke of an oar, and a booming voice calling, "Kick yo' feet, chile!"

AUTHOR'S NOTE

The Legacy Continues. . . .

Part proceeds from sales of *Our Friend Joe* are being donated to the Lifesaving Society/Société de Sauvetage.

For over one hundred years, the Lifesaving Society/Société de Sauvetage (formerly the Royal Life Saving Society) has been the national institute for lifeguarding expertise in Canada. It is a not-for-profit organization, whose mandate is to reduce water-related death and injury through lifesaving training, Water Smart® public education, aquatic safety management services and lifesaving competitions. Each year, over seven hundred thousand participants Canada-wide receive certification through Lifesaving Society/Société de Sauvetage programs.

We think that Joe would have been pleased with this arrangement. Therefore on behalf of Joe and the Lifesaving Society/Société de Sauvetage:

Thank you for your support!

NOTES

FEBRUARY 7, 1922 (pp. 1–2)

1 Mary Elizabeth Colman, "English Bay Joe Was Our First Life-guard," *Vancouver Province*, August 23, 1952, 16.

CHAPTER 1: TRINIDADIAN HERITAGE (pp. 3–7)

1 *Census of Canada, 1891*. Census Place: Vancouver City, New West-minster, British Columbia, Page 11, Row 5. www.collections canada.gc.ca/ (accessed December 2011).

2 *Census of Canada, 1901*. Census Place: Vancouver City, Burrard, British Columbia, Page 2, Row 23. www.collectionscanada.gc.ca/ (accessed December 2011).

3 *Census of Canada, 1911*. Census Place: Vancouver City, Page 12, Line 30. www.collectionscanada.gc.ca/ (accessed December 2011).

4 Donald Wood, *Trinidad in Transition: The Years after Slavery* (New York: Oxford University Press, 1968), 31–32.

5 Bridget Brereton, *A History of Modern Trinidad 1783–1962* (Port of Spain: Heinemann Education Books Caribbean, 1981), 84.

6 Donald Wood, *Trinidad in Transition*, 228–29.

7 St. Mary's College, "The History of the College. The First One Hundred Years: 1863–1963." http://stmarys.edu.tt/ (accessed May 2008).

8 "Fortes, Joe," City of Vancouver Archives, Major Matthews Collection, Microfiche #AM0054.013.01558.

CHAPTER 2: LIVERPOOL YEARS (pp. 9–16)

1 Goldvine Howard, "Joe Fortes of English Bay," *B.C. Historical News*, Vol. 24 (Vancouver: B.C. Historical Society, Fall 1991), 16–18.

2 Noel Robinson, "Joe Fortes, Children's Friend (An Appreciation)," Vancouver: Vancouver City Archives Newspaper Clippings re: Joe Fortes 1922; 1952, Loc. 547-C-6 file 33.

3 "Long and Honorable Career Appreciated," *Vancouver Daily News-Advertiser*, December 23, 1910, 2.

4 Noel Robinson, "The Story of My Life: Joe Fortes," *Vancouver Daily News-Advertiser*, January 19, 1913, 9.

5 Mary Elizabeth Colman, "English Bay Joe Was Our First Lifeguard," *Vancouver Province*, August 23, 1952, 16.

6 *The Public Baths*, Liverpool Record Office, Liverpool Fq 1003.

7 Noel Robinson, "The Story of My Life: Joe Fortes," 9.

8 Tom Slemen, "Tales from the Past," *Liverpool Echo*, July 30, 2005, 2.

9 Noel Robinson, "The Story of My Life: Joe Fortes," 9.

10 Noel Robinson, "Joe Fortes, Children's Friend (An Appreciation)," Loc. 547-C-6 file 33.

11 Centennial Temperance Conference, *One Hundred Years of Temperance: A Memorial Volume of the Centennial Temperance Conference held in Philadelphia, PA, September, 1885* (New York: National Temperance Society and Publication House, 1886), 411.

12 David Lewis, *The Churches of Liverpool* (Liverpool: The Bluecoat Press, 2001), 17.

CHAPTER 3: ABOARD THE *ROBERT KERR* (pp. 17–25)

1 Robert Kerr fonds 1884–1885, in Vancouver City Archives, Loc. 501-F-3 (Section 1) inside front cover.

2 Robert Kerr fonds (Section 1), 47.

3 Robert Kerr fonds (Section 1), 65.

4 Robert Kerr fonds (Section 1), 76.

5 Robert Kerr fonds (Section 1), 77.

6 Robert Kerr fonds (Section 1), 80.

7 Robert Kerr fonds (Section 1), 83.

8 Robert Kerr fonds (Section 1), 91.

9 Robert Kerr fonds (Section 1), 122.

10 Robert Kerr fonds (Section 1), 123.

11 Robert Kerr fonds (Section 1), 126.

12 Robert Kerr fonds (Section 1), 148.

13 Robert Kerr fonds (Section 2), 1.

14 Robert Kerr fonds (Section 2), 35.

15 Robert Kerr fonds (Section 2), 40.

16 Robert Kerr fonds (Section 2), 70.

17 Robert Kerr fonds (Section 2), 71.

18 Robert Kerr fonds (Section 2), 72.

19 Robert Kerr fonds (Section 2), 73.

20 Robert Kerr fonds (Section 2), 76.

21 Robert Kerr fonds (Section 2), 94.

22 Robert Kerr fonds (Section 2), 96.

23 Robert Kerr fonds (Section 2), 101.

24 Robert Kerr fonds (Section 3), 1.

25 Robert Kerr fonds (Section 3), 2.

26 Robert Kerr fonds (Section 3), 2.

27 Robert Kerr fonds (Section 3), 4.

28 Robert Kerr fonds (Section 3), 5.

CHAPTER 4: ODD JOB MAN (pp. 27–32)

1 Noel Robinson, "The Story of My Life: Joe Fortes," 9.

2 Robert Kerr fonds (Section 3), 10.

3 Noel Robinson, "The Story of My Life: Joe Fortes," 9.

4 "Fortes, Joe," City of Vancouver Archives, Major Matthews Collection, Microfiche #AM0054.013.01558.

5 "Seraphim," www.seraphim.com/ (accessed October 2011).

6 Noel Robinson, "Joe Fortes, Children's Friend (An Appreciation)," Loc. 547-C-6 file 33).

7 *Vancouver Daily News-Advertiser*, June 8, 1886, 1.

8 Eric Nicol, *Vancouver: The Romance of Canadian Cities Series* (Doubleday Canada: Toronto, 1970), 51.

CHAPTER 5: INFERNO AND RENEWAL (pp. 33–37)

1 Major James Skitt Matthews, *Early Vancouver, Volume Two* (Vancouver: City of Vancouver, 2011), 251.

2 Peter S.N. Claydon & Valerie Melanson, *Vancouver Voters, 1886: A Biographical Dictionary* (Richmond: B.C. Genealogical Society, 1994), 352.

3 Archives Society of Vancouver, *Vancouver Historical Journal*, No. 1–3 (1958–60), 53.

4 "Vancouver's Leviathan," *Vancouver News*, August 4, 1886, 1.

5 Noel Robinson, "The Story of My Life: Joe Fortes," 9.

6 "The Fire By-Law," *Vancouver News*, July 24, 1886, 1.

7 "Ocean to Ocean," *Vancouver Daily News-Advertiser*, May 24, 1887, 1.

8 The Solon Law Archive, Canadian Constitutional Documents, *British Columbia Terms of Union*, Court at Windsor, May 16, 1871, www.solon.org/ (accessed October 2011).

CHAPTER 6: THE PERFECT PLACE (pp. 39–43)

1 "Long and Honorable Career Appreciated," *Vancouver Daily News-Advertiser*, December 23, 1910, 2.

2 Noel Robinson, "The Story of My Life: Joe Fortes," 9.

3 Noel Robinson, "The Story of My Life: Joe Fortes," 9.

4 Samuel Bawlf, *The Secret Voyage of Sir Francis Drake 1577–1580* (Vancouver: Douglas and McIntyre, 2003), 301–02.

5 Terry Spence, *B.C. Yesterday* (Burnaby: Forest Lawn, c. 1960), unpaged.

6 Bruce Macdonald, *Vancouver: A Visual History* (Vancouver: Talonbooks, 1992), cover map.

CHAPTER 7: BARTENDER STANDARDS (pp. 45–50)

1 Noel Robinson, "Joe Fortes, Children's Friend (An Appreciation)," Loc. 547-C-6 file 33.

2 Anne Kloppenburg, Alice Niwinski, Eve Johnson & Robert Gruetter, *Vancouver's First Century: A City Album 1860–1960* (North Vancouver: J.J. Douglas, 1977), 55.

3 Aileen Campbell, "All Their Yesterdays," *Vancouver Province*, May 28, 1976, 38.

4 "A gloom seemed to pervade . . . ," *Vancouver Daily News-Advertiser*, August 31, 1888, 8.

5 "The announcement that Mr. Joseph Fortz . . . ," *Vancouver Daily News-Advertiser*, September 1, 1888, 8.

6 James Skitt Matthews, *Early Vancouver, Volume 2* (Vancouver: City of Vancouver, 2011), 304–05.

7 City Council and Office of the City Clerk fonds in Vancouver City Archives, *By-Law No. 135: The Vagrancy By-Law*, Loc. 29-A-3 folder 2.

CHAPTER 8: GUARDIAN, TEACHER AND FRIEND (pp. 51–57)

1 Alan Morley, *Vancouver: From Milltown to Metropolis* (Vancouver: Mitchell Press, 1961), 156.

2 Scurry/Howard family history obtained in conversation with Barbara Howard, Burnaby, B.C., January 17, 2011.

3 Goldvine Howard, "Joe Fortes of English Bay," *B.C. Historical News*, Vol. 24 (Fall 1991), 16–18.

4 Scurry/Howard family history obtained in conversation with Barbara Howard, Burnaby, B.C., January 17, 2011.

5 Charlotte Gray, *Gold Diggers: Striking it Rich in the Klondike* (Toronto: HarperCollins, 2010), 38–41.

6 "News of Vancouver," *Daily Colonist*, June 8, 1898, 6.

CHAPTER 9: THE ANGEL AND THE PIRATES (pp. 59–63)

1 Thomas à Kempis, *The Imitation of Christ* (New York: Vintage Books, 1998), 111.

2 Archdiocese of Vancouver, *Traditions of Faith and Service* (Vancouver: The Archdiocese of Vancouver, 2008), 175.

3 "History of the Bells," Vancouver: Holy Rosary Cathedral brochure.

4 Vancouver City Archives, *City Council Minutes*, Vol. 9, May 21, 1900, 627.

5 "Joe Fortes, Veteran Life Guard, Is Kiddies Friend," *Vancouver Sun*, November 9, 1919, 6.

6 Vancouver City Archives, *City Council Minutes*, Vol. 9, June 1, 1900, 647.

7 William Heilbron, "Joe Knew Kids, Piracy: English Bay Version," *Vancouver Province*, February 11, 1961, 15.

CHAPTER 10: TRIUMPHS AND TRIBULATIONS (pp. 65–74)

1 "Rescued From Death: Joe Fortes, Swimming Master, Saves a Little Boy," *Vancouver Daily Province*, June 16, 1900, 1.

2 "Should Have the Medal," *Vancouver Daily Province*, August 25, 1900, 1.

3 James Skitt Matthews, *Early Vancouver, Volume One* (Vancouver: City of Vancouver, 2011), 71.

4 "Letters to the Editor: Continuance of Joe Fortes," *Vancouver Daily Province*, October 15, 1900, 6.

5 "Letters to the Editor: Joe Fortes Again," *Vancouver Daily Province*, October 19, 1900, 3.

6 "Letters to the Editor: The Voice of a Friend," *Vancouver Daily Province*, October 20, 1900, 11.

7 "Letters to the Editor: Joe Fortes Again," *Vancouver Daily Province*, October 20, 1900, 11.

8 Roy Brown, "Joe Fortes, English Bay 'Señor' Was Greatly Beloved Figure," *Vancouver Sun*, May 12, 1954, 5.

9 Vancouver City Archives, *Police and Fire Committee Minutes*, Vol. 10, April 9, 1901, 145.

10 "Council and the Board: Neelands and Joe Fortes," *Vancouver Daily Province*, April 16, 1901, 2.

11 City Council and Office of the City Clerk's fonds, "Petitions re Joe Fortes," in Vancouver Archives, Loc. 594-B-5 file 34.

12 Vancouver City Archives, *City Council Minutes*, Vol. 12, March 21, 1904, 285.

13 Vancouver City Archives, *City Council Finance Committee Minutes*, Vol.12, May 6, 1904, 419.

14 "Saved Boy from Drowning: Joe Fortes Adds Another to His List of Rescues," *Vancouver Daily Province*, May 31, 1904, 1.

15 Vancouver City Archives, *City Council Finance Committee Minutes*, Vol. 13, October 28, 1904, 11.

16 Vancouver City Archives, *City Council Minutes*, Vol.13, November 8, 1904, 25.

17 Vancouver City Archives, *City Council Minutes*, Vol. 13, November 11, 1904, 32.

18 Vancouver City Archives, *City Council Minutes*, Vol. 13, December 2, 1904, 68.

19 Vancouver City Archives, *City Council Minutes*, Vol. 13, December 9, 1904, 80.

CHAPTER 11: A NEW HOME (pp. 75–81)

1 "Willie Dalton, Friend of English Bay, 75 Tomorrow," Annie Dalton fonds clipping, I.K. Barber Learning Centre, University of British Columbia, Rare Books and Special Collections. No call number available, Box 1-11.

2 Vancouver City Archives, *City Council Minutes*, Vol. 13, April 7, 1905, 327.

3 *Henderson's City of Vancouver Directory 1906*, 44.

4 "Fortes Pluck," *Vancouver Daily Province*, August 2, 1905, 1.

CHAPTER 12: RIGHTS AND RACISM (pp. 83–87)

1 "Interesting Questions Regarding English Bay Improvements Discussed by Park Commissioners," *Vancouver Daily Province*, April 12, 1906, 13.

2 "Joe Fortes Had Busy Day," *Vancouver Daily Province*, June 4, 1906, 1.

3 "Joe Fortes Poses as a Legal Light," *Vancouver Daily Province*, June 28, 1907, 14.

CHAPTER 13: TRIUMPH AND TRAGEDY (pp. 89–96)

1 "Plucky Joe Fortes Makes Brave Rescue," *Vancouver Daily Province*, March 3, 1908, 1.

2 Vancouver City Archives, *City Council Minutes*, Vol. 15, April 2, 1908, 271.

3 "Young Women Are Drowned at Bay," *Vancouver Daily Province*, July 13, 1908, 1.

4 "The Sea Gives Up Its Dead," *Vancouver Daily News-Advertiser*, July 15, 1908, 1–2.

5 "Two Lives Lost at English Bay," *Vancouver Daily New-Advertiser*, July 13, 1908, 2.

6 "Gold Medal for 'Joe' Fortes," *Vancouver World*, July 22, 1908, 2.

7 "Honor Joe Fortes for Noble Work," *Vancouver Daily Province*, July 22, 1908, 5.

8 "Joe Fortes Is Himself Again," *Vancouver Daily News-Advertiser*, July 24, 1908, 4.

9 "Well Defined Channel along English Bay Beach," *Vancouver Daily Province*, July 24, 1908, 18.

10 "Joe Fortes Is Himself Again," 4.

11 "Well Defined Channel along English Bay Beach," 18.

CHAPTER 14: "MERRY CHRISTMAS, JOE!" (pp. 97–104)

1 "Bathing Pavilion an Attraction," *Vancouver Daily Province*, February 13, 1909, 18.

2 "Long and Honorable Career Appreciated," *Vancouver Daily News-Advertiser*, December 23, 1910, 21.

3 "Mr. Joseph Fortes, swimming instructor and life saver," original certificate at Old Hastings Mill Store Museum, 1575 Alma Street, Vancouver, B.C. Owned and operated by Native Daughters of B.C. Post #1.

4 Noel Robinson, "The Story of My Life: Joe Fortes," 9.

CHAPTER 15: LIFE GOES ON (pp. 105–14)

1 Scurry/Howard family history obtained in conversation with Barbara Howard, Burnaby, B.C., January 17, 2011.

2 W.S. Rawlings, *First Annual Report of the Board of Park Commissioners, Vancouver, British Columbia* (Vancouver Board of Park Commissioners, 1911–1915), 25.

3 W.S. Rawlings, *First Annual Report of the Board of Park Commissioners, Vancouver, British Columbia*, 72.

4 "Hero Buried with Military Ceremonies," *Vancouver Daily World*, April 1, 1912, 1.

5 Alan Hustak, *Titanic: The Canadian Story* (Montreal: Véhicule Press, 1999).

6 Correspondence: Simpson Brother's application for boating and bathing lease, Apr. 1912–Dec. 1913 (Vancouver: Vancouver Board of Parks and Recreation fonds, in Vancouver City Archives Loc. 48-C-3, folder 4).

7 Noel Robinson, "The Story of My Life: Joe Fortes," 9.

CHAPTER 16: HOME FIRES (pp. 115–21)

1 Vancouver City Archives, *Vancouver Park Board, Public Utilities Committee Minutes MCR 48-1, 1912–1949*, May 11, 1915, 259.

2 Vancouver City Archives, *Vancouver Park Board, Public Utilities Committee Minutes MCR 48-1, 1912–1949*, May 21, 1915, 261.

3 Vancouver City Archives, *Vancouver Park Board, Public Utilities Committee Minutes MCR 48-1, 1912–1949*, May 21, 1915, 260.

4 Vancouver City Archives, *Vancouver Park Board, Public Utilities Committee Minutes MCR 48-1, 1912–1949*, July 12, 1915, 267.

5 "Vice-Regal Party Had Very Busy Day," *Vancouver Daily Province*, July 20, 1916, 16.

6 "Interviewing Joe Fortes and the Two Tides which Roll across English Bay Beach," *Vancouver Daily Province*, August 30, 1916, 3.

7 "Interviewing Joe Fortes and the Two Tides which Roll across English Bay Beach," *Vancouver Daily Province*, August 30, 1916, 3.

CHAPTER 17: THE BRACELET (pp. 123–26)

1 Goldvine Howard, "Joe Fortes of English Bay," *B.C. Historical News*, Vol. 24 (Fall 1991): 16–18.

2 Scurry/Howard family history obtained in conversation with Barbara Howard, Burnaby, B.C., January 17, 2011.

CHAPTER 18: DECLINE (pp. 127–32)

1 Vancouver City Archives, *Committee of the Whole Board Minutes MCR 48-1, 1912–1949*, March 25, 1918, unpaged.

2 Vancouver City Archives, *City Council Minutes*, Vol. 22, May 14, 1919, 483.

3 "Joe Fortes, Veteran Life Guard, Is Kiddies Friend," *Vancouver Sun*, November 9, 1919, 6.

4 Vancouver Polar Bear Swim Club, "Brief History of the Vancouver Polar Bear Swim," http://vancouver.ca/parks/ (accessed October 2011).

5 Joe's walking cane is displayed at Vancouver Public Library Joe Fortes Branch, 870 Denman Street, Vancouver, B.C., V6G 2L8.

6 Michael Kluckner, *Vancouver Remembered* (Vancouver: Whitecap Books, 2006), 132.

7 "Joe Fortes Taken to the Hospital," *Vancouver Daily Province*, January 17, 1922, 2.

8 "'Old Joe' Is Taken to the Hospital," *Vancouver Sun*, January 17, 1922, 1.

9 "'Ah'm Alright' Says Joe, But Doctors Keep Him," *Vancouver Daily Province*, January 18, 1922, 2.

CHAPTER 19: "THE PASSING OF A GREAT SOUL" (pp. 133–38)

1 Goldvine Howard, "Joe Fortes of English Bay" *B.C. Historical News*, Vol. 24, (Vancouver: B.C. Historical Society: Fall 1991), 16–18.

2 John Henry Newman, "Lead, Kindly Light," 1833, www.oremus.org/ (accessed September 2008).

3 Vancouver City Archives, *City Council Minutes*, Vol. 23, February 6, 1922, 686.

4 "Entire City Will Pay Its Respects to Warm-Hearted 'Joe' Fortes," *Vancouver Sun*, February 6, 1922, 1.

5 "The Funeral of Joe Fortes . . . ," *Vancouver Daily Province*, February 6, 1922, 3.

6 "Thousands Pay Last Tribute," *Vancouver Daily Province*, February 7, 1922, 20.

7 "Thousands Pay Last Tribute," 20.

8 The Joe Fortes grave is located at Mountain View Cemetery, City of Vancouver, Grave marker 1919–B–40–9.

9 "Thousands Pay Last Tribute," 20.

CHAPTER 20: JOE'S LEGACY (pp. 139–48)

1 Noel Robinson, "Joe Fortes, Children's Friend (An Appreciation)," in Vancouver City Archives Loc. 547-C-6 file 33.

2 *Probate in the Matter of the "Administration Act" and in the Matter of the Estate of Joseph Fortes Deceased*, British Columbia Supreme Court (Vancouver) Probate files, 1893–1941, Call No. 1415.

3 Goldvine Howard, "Joe Fortes of English Bay," *B.C. Historical News*, Vol. 24 (Fall 1991), 16–18.

4 "Heros and Hero Worship," *Vancouver Daily Province*, January 15, 1925, 8.

5 "Boy 'Chips In' for 'Old Joe,'" *Vancouver Daily Province*, April 6, 1926, 26.

6 "Proposed Memorial in Honor of the Late Joe Fortes," *Vancouver Daily Province*, February 15, 1926, 1.

7 "Unveil Bronze Memorial to City's Beloved Life Guard," *Vancouver Daily Province*, June 25, 1927, 18.

8 "Vancouver Historical Society, Citizen of the Century," *Vancouver Historical Society Newsletter*, Vancouver, May 1986, 1.

9 "Grave Marker is Tribute in Stone to Gentle Giant," *Vancouver Sun*, September 21, 2005, B1, B4.

10 Ian Nicholson, "Joe Fortes: Little Children Loved Him," *Vancouver Daily Province Magazine Section*, July 19, 1947, 7.

11 Mary Elizabeth Colman, "English Bay Joe Was Our First Lifeguard," *Vancouver Province*, August 23, 1952, 16.

12 Gregory Bangs, "The Real Old Black Joe," *Daily Colonist*, September 28, 1975, 3.

13 Frank Farley, "Lifeguard Joe Fortes Still Remembered," *Vancouver Province*, March 18, 1964, 4.

14 Chuck Bayley, "A Legend Lives On: One of Vancouver's Best-loved Heroes Remembered," *Vancouver Sun*, November 19, 1985, B2.

15 Chuck Bayley, B2.

16 Chuck Bayley, B2.

17 Betty McLean, "Joe Fortes, The Lamp Lighter," Rootsweb, http://freepages.family.rootsweb.ancestry.com/ (accessed October 2011).

18 Hugh Pickett's reminiscences of Joe obtained in telephone interview, Vancouver, 2004.

19 Renee Jensen, *Reminiscences of Renee Jensen* (Vancouver: Joe Fortes Library).

BIBLIOGRAPHY

PRIMARY SOURCES

British Columbia Archives
Probate case files

City of Vancouver Archives
Vancouver City Council Minutes
Vancouver Park Board Minutes
Vancouver Park Board Annual Report 1911
Major Matthews Topical Files, Volumes 1–6
Log of the *Robert Kerr*, 1884–1885
Petitions re: Joe Fortes
Newspaper clippings re: Joe Fortes
Robinson, Noel: Major Matthews collection
Charles Marega fonds
Stanley H. Warn fonds
Correspondence: Simpson Brothers Application for Boating & Bathing
    Lease Apr. 1912–Dec. 1913

Vancouver Public Library
Government of Canada Census records 1891, 1901, 1911
B.C. Civil Registration Records: Death Registrations
Henderson's City of Vancouver Directories
Williams Vancouver and New Westminster Cities Directory
British Columbia Directory, R.T. Williams, Publisher, W.M. Wolz,
    Compiler

Vancouver Voters, 1886: A Biographical Dictionary, edited and compiled by Peter S.N. Claydon, Valerie Melanson, members of the B.C. Genealogical Society

Native Daughters of B.C. Post #1
City of Vancouver Illuminated Address: Joseph Fortes

University of British Columbia: I.K. Barber Learning Centre
Annie Dalton fonds

Holy Rosary Cathedral Priory
Deaths Registrum Defunctorum Ecclesiae

Newspapers
Times Colonist
Vancouver Daily Advertiser
Vancouver Daily News-Advertiser
Vancouver Daily Province
Vancouver Daily World
Vancouver News
Vancouver Province
Vancouver Sun
The West Ender

PUBLISHED SOURCES

à Kempis, Thomas. *The Imitation of Christ in Four Books*. New York, NY: Vintage Books, 1998.

Abranson, Erik. *Sailors of the Great Sailing Ships*. London, U.K.: Macdonald Educational, 1978.

Barnholden, Michael. *Reading the Riot Act*. Vancouver, B.C.: Anvil Press, 2005.

Barman, Jean. *Stanley Park's Secret*. Madeira Park, B.C.: Harbour Publishing, 2005.

Bawlf, Samuel. *The Secret Voyage of Sir Francis Drake 1577–1580*. Vancouver, B.C.: Douglas and McIntyre, 2003.

Brereton, Bridget. *A History of Modern Trinidad 1783–1962*. Port-of-Spain: Heinemann Educational Books (Caribbean), 1981.

"Brief History of the Vancouver Polar Bear Swim." In Vancouver Board of Parks and Recreation, online at http://vancouver.ca/parks/ (accessed October 2011).

"Canada and the First World War." In Canadian War Museum, online at www.warmuseum.ca/ (accessed April 2011).

"Canada's Naval History: Explore History, First World War (1914–1918)." In Canadian War Museum, online at www.warmuseum.ca/ (accessed April 2011).

Caple, Kenneth. "A Small Boy's West End." *Vancouver Historical Society Newsletter*, April 1977.

The Cathedral of Our Lady of the Holy Rosary: History of the Cathedral, 1885–2000. Vancouver, B.C.: Holy Rosary Parish, no date.

Census of Canada, 1891. In Library and Archives Canada, online at www.collectionscanada.gc.ca/ (accessed December 2011).

Census of Canada, 1901. In Library and Archives Canada, online at www.collectionscanada.gc.ca/ (accessed December 2011).

Census of Canada, 1911. In Library and Archives Canada, online at www.collectionscanada.gc.ca/ (accessed December 2011).

Centennial Temperance Conference. *One Hundred Years of Temperance: A Memorial Volume of the Centennial Temperance Conference Held in Philadelphia, PA, September, 1885*. New York, NY: National Temperance Society and Publication House, 1886.

"Charles Marega." In *The History of Metropolitan Vancouver*, online at www.vancouverhistory.ca/archives_marega.htm (accessed January 2008).

Claydon, Peter S.N. & Valerie Melanson. *Vancouver Voters, 1886: A Biographical Dictionary*. Richmond, B.C.: B.C. Genealogical Society, 1994.

Cohen, Stan. *The Streets Were Paved with Gold: A Pictorial History of the Klondike Gold Rush 1896–1899*. Missoula, MT: Sagebrush Education Resources, 1977.

Colwin, Cecil. *Breakthrough Swimming*. Champaign, IL: Human Kinetics, 2002.

Conn, Heather & Henry Ewert. *Vancouver's Glory Years: Public Transit, 1890–1915*. North Vancouver, B.C.: Whitecap Books, 2003.

Cunard Home Page. Online at www.chriscunard.com/ (accessed April 2009).

Davis, Chuck. "A Year in Five Minutes: Vancouver, 1914." *Re:place Magazine*, online at http://regardingplace.com/ (accessed April 2011).

———, ed. *The Greater Vancouver Book: An Urban Encyclopedia*. Surrey, B.C.: Linkman Press, 1997.

———. *The History of Metropolitan Vancouver*, online at www.vancouverhistory.ca/ (accessed January 2008).

Donahue, Mary. "History of Lifesaving," online at http://faculty.deanza.edu/donahuemary/Historyoflifesaving (accessed November 2009).

"Esquimalt History: From Early First Nations Presence to Today." In Township of Esquimalt, online at www.esquimalt.ca/ (accessed May 2009).

Ewert, Henry. *The Story of the B.C. Electric Company*. North Vancouver, B.C.: Whitecap Books, 1986.

"Eyewitness to History: Assassination of Archduke Ferdinand, 1914." Online at www.eyewitnesstohistory.com/duke.htm (accessed April 2011).

Goad, Charles E. *Goad's Atlas (Fire Insurance Plans), City of Vancouver and Vicinity*, 1912. Map 342, Plate 145.

Golden Jubilee Program: Cathedral of Our Lady of the Holy Rosary. Vancouver, B.C.: Holy Rosary Parish, December 8, 1950.

Government of the Republic of Trinidad and Tobago, online at www.ttconnect.gov.tt/ (accessed April 2008).

Gray, Charlotte. *Gold Diggers: Striking it Rich in the Klondike*. Toronto, ON: HarperCollins, 2010.

Green, Valerie. "A Classic by the Bay." In *Senior Living Magazine*, online at http://seniorlivingmagazine.com/ (accessed February 2012).

Greer, Rosamond. "English Bay Joe." *Westworld Magazine*, January/February 1979.

Gresko, Jacqueline. *Traditions of Faith and Service: Archdiocese of Vancouver 1908–2008*. Vancouver, B.C.: Archdiocese of Vancouver, 2008.

Hayes, Derek. *Historical Atlas of Vancouver and the Lower Fraser Valley*. Vancouver, B.C.: Douglas and McIntyre, 2005.

"History of English Bay." Online at http://englishbay.com/history ofeb.html (accessed November 2009).

"History of Swimming." Online at http://home.comcast.net/~hot_tub/history-of-swimming.htm (accessed March 2009).

Howard, Goldvine. "Joe Fortes of English Bay." *B.C. Historical News*, Vol. 24 (Fall, 1991).

Hustak, Alan. "Titanic: The Canadian Story." In Encyclopedia Titanica, online at www.encyclopedia-titanica.org/ (accessed September 2009).

Kloppenburg, Anne, Alice Niwinski, Eve Johnson & Robert Gruetter. *Vancouver's First Century: A City Album 1860–1960*. North Vancouver, B.C.: J.J. Douglas, 1977.

Kluckner, Michael. *Vancouver Remembered*. North Vancouver, B.C.: Whitecap Books, 2006.

———. *Vancouver: The Way It Was, 10th Anniversary Edition*. North Vancouver, B.C.: Whitecap Books, 1993.

Lewis, David. *The Churches of Liverpool*. Liverpool, UK: The Bluecoat Press, 2001.

Lifesaving Society/Société de Sauvetage. Online at www.lifesaving.ca/ (accessed August 2011).

Light, Lois. "The Villages of Stanley Park." *Westworld Magazine*, December 1981.

Liverpool City Council. Online at http://liverpool.gov.uk/ (accessed October 2003).

Liverpool History Society. Online at www.liverpoolhistorysociety.org.uk/ (accessed November 2003).

"Luncheon a Great Success." *Vancouver Historical Society Newsletter*, May 2010, online at www.vancouver-historical-society.ca/ (accessed January 2012).

Macdonald, Bruce. *Vancouver: A Visual History*. Vancouver, B.C.: Talon, 1992.

McLean, Betty. "Joe Fortes, The Lamp Lighter," in Rootsweb, online at http://freepages.family.rootsweb.ancestry.com/ (accessed October 2011).

Matthews, Major James Skitt. *Early Vancouver, Volumes One & Two*. Vancouver, B.C.: Self published, 1932.

————. *Pilot Commander Don José Maria Narvaéz 1791*. Vancouver, B.C.: City Archives, City Hall, Vancouver. July 1, 1941.

Mattison, David. *Eyes of a City: Early Vancouver Photographers 1868–1900*. Vancouver, B.C.: Vancouver City Archives, 1986.

"Medical News: Silvester Traced." In *British Medical Journal*, online at www.ncbi.nlm.nih.gov/ (accessed January 2012).

"Mersey Gateway: An Online History of the Port and Its People." In PortCities Liverpool, online at www.mersey-gateway.org (accessed October 2003).

Morley, Alan. *Vancouver: From Milltown to Metropolis*. Vancouver, B.C.: Mitchell Press, 1961.

National Archives of Trinidad and Tobago. Online at http://natt.gov.tt/ (accessed May 2008).

Newland, J. *Liverpool Baths and Wash Houses*. Report of City Engineer, 1856.

Newman, John Henry. "Lead Kindly Light," in Oremus Hymnal, online at www.oremus.org/ (accessed September 2008).

Nicol, Eric. *Vancouver: The Romance of Canadian Cities Series*. Toronto, ON: Doubleday Canada, 1970.

Pethick, Derek. *Vancouver: The Pioneer Years 1774–1886*. Langley, B.C.: Sunfire Publications, 1984.

"Quarters, Road Districts and Ward Unions (Trinidad)." In Trinidad & Tobago Genealogy, online at www.trinidadandtobagofamily history.org/ (accessed April 2008).

Robinson, Noel. "The Story of My Life: Joe Fortes." *Vancouver Daily News-Advertiser*, January 19, 1913.

Robson, Ethel. *Tales of Vancouver: From Lumber Chips to Computer Chips*. New Westminster, B.C., 1985.

Roy, Patricia E. *Vancouver: An Illustrated History*. Toronto, ON: James Lorimer, 1980.

Sayers, Ivan W. "A Vancouver Story." *Vancouver Museum Muse News,* March/April, c. 1980.

"Seraphim." Online at www.seraphim.com/ (accessed October 2011).

Sleigh, Daphne. *People of the Harrison*. Deroche, B.C.: D. Sleigh, 1990.

Slemen, Tom. "Tales from the Past." *Liverpool Echo*, July 30, 2005, Liverpool, England.

Snyders, Tom & Jennifer O'Rourke. *Namely Vancouver*. Vancouver, B.C.: Arsenal Pulp Press, 2001.

The Solon Law Archive, Canadian Constitutional Documents. *British Columbia Terms of Union*, online at www.solon.org/ (accessed October 2011).

Spence, Terry. *B.C. Yesterday*. Burnaby B.C.: Forest Lawn, c. 1960.

Spray, Laree. "Stanley Park Beaches Have Histories." *Vancouver Daily Province*, September 20, 1941.

"St. Mary's College, Holy Ghost Fathers." Online at http://stmarys. edu.tt (accessed May 2008).

"St. Mary's RC Church, Liverpool: History, Record and Information." In Rootsweb, online at http://freepages.genealogy.rootsweb. ancestry.com/ (accessed March 2009).

Starkins, Edward. *Ayulshun: The Story of English Bay and the West End*. The Research Project on B.C. Photography, Kit #55. Vancouver Public Library, 1974.

Steele, Richard. *The First 100 Years: The Vancouver Board of Parks and Recreation, An Illustrated Celebration*. Vancouver, B.C., 1988.

"Sunken Ships/Shipwrecks." Online at www.thecanadianencyclopedia.com/ (accessed February 2012).

Swan, Staff Sergeant G.M. *A Century of Service: The Vancouver Police 1886–1986*. Vancouver, B.C.: Vancouver Historical Society and Centennial Museum, 1986.

Thirkell, Fred & Bob Scullion. *Frank Gowen's Vancouver 1914–1931*. Victoria, B.C., Heritage House, 2001.

Walton, Peter, ed. *The VGH Story: A History of Vancouver General Hospital*. Vancouver, B.C. 1988.

Whale, Derek. *Bygone Merseyside*. Manchester, United Kingdom: Archive Publications in association with *The Liverpool Echo*, 1989.

Wiseman, Les. "The End." *Vancouver Magazine*, July, 1983.

Wood, Donald. *Trinidad in Transition: The Years after Slavery*. New York, NY: Oxford University Press, 1968.

ABOUT THE AUTHORS

LISA ANNE SMITH is an education docent at the Museum of Vancouver and a member of Native Daughters of B.C. Post #1, owners and operators of the Old Hastings Mill Store Museum—Vancouver's oldest building. She has written a children's book as a fundraiser for the preservation of the RCMP ship the *St. Roch*. She lives with her husband and two grown children in Vancouver.

BARBARA ROGERS has spent many years researching family history as a volunteer archivist for the B.C. Genealogical Society, and has compiled four books for them. Presently at work on a biography of Simon Fraser, she has contributed articles on his life to numerous reference works. She lives in Vancouver.

INDEX

Citations of photographs are in bold.